EASY MONEY

by Arnold Ridley

Copyright © 1948 by Samuel French Ltd
© Revised and rewritten, 1955 by Samuel French Ltd
All Rights Reserved

EASY MONEY is fully protected under the copyright laws of the British Commonwealth, including Canada, the United States of America, and all other countries of the Copyright Union. All rights, including professional and amateur stage productions, recitation, lecturing, public reading, motion picture, radio broadcasting, television, online/digital production, and the rights of translation into foreign languages are strictly reserved.

ISBN 978-0-573-01117-7

concordtheatricals.co.uk
concordtheatricals.com

FOR AMATEUR PRODUCTION ENQUIRIES

UNITED KINGDOM AND WORLD
EXCLUDING NORTH AMERICA
licensing@concordtheatricals.co.uk
020-7054-7298

Each title is subject to availability from Concord Theatricals,
depending upon country of performance.

CAUTION: Professional and amateur producers are hereby warned that *EASY MONEY* is subject to a licensing fee. The purchase, renting, lending or use of this book does not constitute a licence to perform this title(s), which licence must be obtained from the appropriate agent prior to any performance. Performance of this title(s) without a licence is a violation of copyright law and may subject the producer and/or presenter of such performances to penalties. Both amateurs and professionals considering a production are strongly advised to apply to the appropriate agent before starting rehearsals, advertising, or booking a theatre. A licensing fee must be paid whether the title is presented for charity or gain and whether or not admission is charged.

This work is published by Samuel French, an imprint of Concord Theatricals Ltd.

The Professional Rights in this play are controlled by Concord Theatricals, Aldwych House, 71-91 Aldwych, London, WC2B 4HN, UK.

No one shall make any changes in this title for the purpose of production. No part of this book may be reproduced, stored in a retrieval system, scanned, uploaded, or transmitted in any form, by any means, now known or yet to be invented, including mechanical, electronic, digital, photocopying, recording, videotaping, or otherwise, without the prior written permission of the publisher. No one shall share this title, or part of this title, to any social media or file hosting websites.

The moral right of Arnold Ridley to be identified as author of this work has been asserted in accordance with Section 77 of the Copyright, Designs and Patents Act 1988.

USE OF COPYRIGHTED MUSIC

A licence issued by Concord Theatricals to perform this play does not include permission to use the incidental music specified in this publication. In the United Kingdom: Where the place of performance is already licensed by the PERFORMING RIGHT SOCIETY (PRS) a return of the music used must be made to them. If the place of performance is not so licensed then application should be made to PRS for Music (www.prsformusic.com). A separate and additional licence from PHONOGRAPHIC PERFORMANCE LTD (www.ppluk.com) may be needed whenever commercial recordings are used. Outside the United Kingdom: Please contact the appropriate music licensing authority in your territory for the rights to any incidental music.

USE OF COPYRIGHTED THIRD-PARTY MATERIALS

Licensees are solely responsible for obtaining formal written permission from copyright owners to use copyrighted third-party materials (e.g., artworks, logos) in the performance of this play and are strongly cautioned to do so. If no such permission is obtained by the licensee, then the licensee must use only original materials that the licensee owns and controls. Licensees are solely responsible and liable for clearances of all third-party copyrighted materials, and shall indemnify the copyright owners of the play(s) and their licensing agent, Concord Theatricals Ltd., against any costs, expenses, losses and liabilities arising from the use of such copyrighted third-party materials by licensees.

IMPORTANT BILLING AND CREDIT REQUIREMENTS

If you have obtained performance rights to this title, please refer to your licensing agreement for important billing and credit requirements.

EASY MONEY

First produced at the Grand Theatre, Blackpool, on Monday, 24th February 1947, with the following cast of characters:

(in the order of their appearance)

GRANDMA STAFFORD	*Dorothy Dewhurst*
JACQUELINE WORRALL (JACKY)	*Jane Holland*
RUTH STAFFORD	*René Kelly*
PHILIP STAFFORD	*Arnold Ridley*
CAROL STAFFORD	*Honor Shepherd*
DENIS STAFFORD	*Victor Adams*
MARTHA	*Rhodda Beresford*
MARTIN LATHAM	*John Hewitt*
GEORGE KIRBY	*Nicholas Grimshaw*

The play directed by OLIVER GORDON

SYNOPSIS OF SCENES

The action of the play takes place in the lounge of Philip Stafford's house situated on the outskirts of Caterham-on-the-Hill, Surrey, in Winter. The time is the present

ACT I
Saturday evening

ACT II
Sunday morning

ACT III
Monday evening

EASY MONEY

ACT I

SCENE—*The lounge of Philip Stafford's house at Caterham-on-the-Hill, Surrey.*
In every house inhabited by the family of a retired business man of moderate means there is usually a room described as the "lounge" which supplies a variety of needs. Sometimes it is used as a dining-room (to save fires); sometimes for the entertainment of guests, but, more often, as a general hunting ground for all and sundry. It is such a room in the detached residence of Philip Stafford (a retired wine merchant), situated near Caterham, in Surrey, that provides the scene of the play.
There is nothing remarkable about "the lounge". It is comfortably, if rather untidily, furnished in a chintzy sort of way, and it is obviously used by various members of the family in a different capacity. The fireplace is R and above it stands an easy chair. Then, set on an angle, there is a french window leading up to the back wall which consists largely of bookshelves. The door LC faces the audience, and in the right-hand corner stands a large radiogram. A small door down L leads to "the study". There is a large settee RC, a round table C, and various "supporting" furniture.
(See the Ground Plan at the end of the Play)

When the CURTAIN *rises, it is about five o'clock on a Saturday evening in late December. The room is empty, and the only illumination comes from the fire, which is burning brightly, and a grey twilight from the window.*
After a pause, the door up L *opens and* MARTHA, *an elderly maid-servant, enters carrying a tea-tray. She places this on the radiogram, switches on the lights, crosses the room, closes the chintz curtains and then places the tray on the table which has already been laid for tea. She takes a glance at the fire and, finding presumably that it is burning to her satisfaction, quits the room.*
There is another short pause and then HARRIET STAFFORD (GRANDMA) *comes in up* L. GRANDMA *is about seventy-five and poses as a "dear old lady", but—well, ask the Staffords. She is dressed in mauve and black and wears a lace cap. She looks cautiously around the room and, finding it empty, approaches the tea-table and regards it closely with greedy interest. She snatches a small bun which she quickly consumes with obvious relish, and in a manner rather resembling a rabbit. Then she grabs a second bun, and retires with it in the direction of the fire. As she does so, the door opens and* JACQUELINE WORRAL *enters and tiptoes across to Grandma.* JACKY *is a bird-like girl of about fifteen, wearing a gym suit. She creeps up behind Grandma on tiptoe.*

JACKY. Stick 'em up!
GRANDMA (*very startled*) Oh! Who's that?
JACKY. It's me! Blonde Bella, the Moll of Two-Gun Nick!
GRANDMA. Oh, it's you, is it? How dare you play tricks like that? You gave me an awful start! (*She sits in the chair above the fire*)
JACKY. Guilty conscience, perhaps?
GRANDMA. Eh?
JACKY (*turning back to above the table and giving it the once-over*) Buns! Hooray! (*She counts them*) Uncle Phil—Aunt Ruth—Denis—Carol—You—Me! Two short! Someone will have to go without besides you, Grandma!
GRANDMA. What do you mean?
JACKY. Well, you've had yours, haven't you?
GRANDMA. Young girls shouldn't speak until they're spoken to.
JACKY. And old girls shouldn't speak with their mouths full.
GRANDMA (*furious*) Well, of all the——
JACKY. Sorry, Grandma.
GRANDMA. And don't call me "Grandma". I'm not your grandmother. I'd have seen that any child of mine brought you up better.
JACKY (*seriously*) Sez you!
GRANDMA. And don't use those ridiculous expressions you learn at the bioscope.
JACKY (*crossing to the fire, kneeling and warming her hands*) Bioscope? Oh, you mean flicks?
GRANDMA. You know perfectly well what I mean. For the life of me, I can't understand why Philip is always giving you money to spend in these disgusting picture palaces—especially as he can't afford it. I've even spoken to your Aunt Ruth about it, but nothing happens.
JACKY. I expect she's forgotten about it. Aunt Ruth doesn't remember things for very long, does she?
RUTH (*off*) Martha! Martha!
JACKY. There she is now.

(RUTH *enters up* L. *She is about fifty and is one of those indefinite and fussy women with a genius for confusing even the simplest of issues. She is carrying a bunch of letters*)

RUTH (*moving to above the table*) Oh, here you are, Jacky. Have you seen Martha?
JACKY. Not lately, Aunt Ruth.
RUTH. Dear me, where can she be? (*As she goes up to the door*) Martha! Martha! I wanted to tell her we'd have tea in here. When did you see her last?
JACKY. When she brought it in.
RUTH. Brought what in?
JACKY. The tea.
RUTH. Oh, she's brought it? (*She calls off*) Martha! (*She comes*

down stage) Oh, then, I don't want her now, do I? How silly of me. (*She moves to the desk and puts down the letters*) What a blessing tea's in.
JACKY. Yes. Grandma's had hers.
GRANDMA. What!
JACKY. Part of it.
RUTH. Has anyone seen Philip? Or Carol? Or Denis?
JACKY (*rising*) Uncle Philip came in five minutes ago. I heard him go into the what's-it.
GRANDMA (*in horror*) Really!
JACKY. Bathroom, then.
RUTH. Then he'll be here soon.
JACKY (*kneeling on the sofa and facing Ruth over the back*) And Carol's playing hockey and Denis has gone to see his friend, Eric Tranter.
RUTH (*remembering*) Oh, yes, of course. (*She moves towards the table*) In that case, we'll begin.
JACKY. Grandma has.
RUTH (*sitting above the table*) Has what, dear?
JACKY. Begun. (*She comes to the table, sits R of it, and reaches for a bun*) Do you mind if I have my bun first, Aunt Ruth? I'll have my bread and butter afterwards.
RUTH. Certainly, dear. (*Pouring tea*) But why?
JACKY. I think buns will be found to drop below the target figure.
RUTH. Are you coming to the table, Grandma, or will you stay by the fire?
GRANDMA. I'll stay here. I've no wish to get in anybody's way.
JACKY. I'll tell the cock-eyed world!
RUTH. Jacky, dear, you really mustn't use that silly picture talk. Pass Grandma her cup.
JACKY (*jumping up*) Oke!

(JACKY *takes a cup of tea to* GRANDMA, *who accepts it without thanks*)

RUTH. I wish Philip would hurry up before the tea gets stewed. (*To Jacky*) Call him, dear, will you?
JACKY. No need! Listen—he's just pulled the——
GRANDMA. Oh!
JACKY. Turned on the tap!
RUTH. Jacky! Dear!
JACKY. Sorry, Aunt Ruth! (*She crosses to the table*)
GRANDMA (*sipping noisily*) This tea isn't very sweet.
RUTH. Sorry, Grandma. It's getting to the end of the week—sugar's running low.
GRANDMA. And we know who to thank for that!
JACKY (*sitting R of the table*) Don't thank me. It was a pleasure.

GRANDMA. Really, Ruth. I've never heard of a child that's been so badly brought up. I know your sister and her husband are in Nairobi and she's been left in the hands of strangers, but——

JACKY. Strangers are truer than fiction, eh?

GRANDMA. What *do* they teach you at school?

JACKY. You'd be surprised!

RUTH. Really, Jacky—your manners.

JACKY (*smiling sweetly*) Sorry, Aunt Ruth!

(*The door opens and* PHILIP STAFFORD *enters*. PHILIP, *who is a retired wine merchant, is a boodling easy-going and kindly man of fifty-seven. He wears an old tweed coat, flannel trousers and a pullover. He seems slightly depressed*)

RUTH. Hello, dear. Come and have your tea.

PHILIP. Not late, am I? Hello, Grandma. Hello, Jacky. Good film?

JACKY. Wizard, Uncle Philip!

PHILIP (*sitting* L *of the table and taking his cup*) Splendid! What was it about?

JACKY. Lurv!

RUTH. Lurv? Oh, you mean love?

JACKY. No, Aunt Ruth—lurv. It was an American film. (*To Philip*) You see, there was a girl. And there were two men. And one of the men loved her and pretended he didn't, and the other one didn't and pretended he did. And the one who did was in the American Marines, and the one who didn't was a spy in the pay of the Reds. And she thought the one who didn't love her did and the one who did didn't, and so she went away with the one who didn't—the one who was a spy—and the one who did, and pretended he didn't—the one in the Marines——

PHILIP (*drily*) Sounds a bit complicated to me.

JACKY. Oh, no, Uncle Philip, quite simple. That was the only fault I found with it—it was a bit obvious. Thank you for letting me go.

PHILIP. Neither Carol nor Denis back yet?

RUTH (*rising and crossing with a plate of food to Grandma*) No. Carol's late. She's playing hockey. (*She returns to the table with Grandma's cup and sits*)

PHILIP. Not in the dark, surely, dear. (*To Jacky*) Where was the game?

JACKY. Godstone.

PHILIP. That's not far.

JACKY. It all depends.

GRANDMA. I suppose she means Carol may have stayed behind to talk to "Mr Right". (*She puts her plate on the table* R *of the armchair*)

JACKY. More likely to be Martin Latham.
GRANDMA. That's what I said.
JACKY. No, you didn't. You said "Mr Right".
RUTH. Jacky, dear, you mustn't contradict. (*She hands Grandma's refilled cup to Jacky*) Grandma means that Mr Latham is "Mr Right".
JACKY (*rising and taking the cup to Grandma*) Funny name for him. I'd call him "Mr Slow". (*She returns to her seat*)

(MARTHA *enters up* L *with a bag of golf clubs*)

MARTHA (*coming down between Ruth and Philip*) Some more hot water, ma'am?
RUTH. Thank you, Martha. I'm afraid you'll have to make fresh for Miss Carol and Mr Denis.
MARTHA. Oh, dear! I forgot! Mr Denis won't be in to tea. He rang to say.
JACKY. Good! Bun situation improves! (*She takes another*)
RUTH. All right, Martha.
MARTHA. Thank you, ma'am. (*She moves to go and then returns to* L *of Philip*) Oh, sir, about your sticks . . .
PHILIP (*puzzled*) Sticks?
MARTHA. Golf sticks, sir. The ones you left in the porch. What would you like me to do with them—hardly safe to leave them outside the front door.
PHILIP (*taking the clubs*) You're quite right, Martha. I'll give them a rub over before I put them away.
MARTHA. Yes, sir.

(MARTHA *goes out up* L *with the hot-water jug*)

RUTH. You usually leave your clubs at the clubhouse, don't you, dear?
PHILIP. Ye-es—usually. (*He rises and stands behind his chair*) I— well, I brought them home instead. (*After a pause*) I'm going to sell them.
RUTH (*surprised*) Sell them?
PHILIP. Yes. (*With false gaiety*) Clubs are fetching a good price these days. I'm going to put an advertisement in the *Sunday Times* next week.
RUTH. I expect you're right, dear, and I hope I'm not being stupid, but if they're as expensive as you say they are, it'll cost you just as much to buy new ones.
PHILIP (*crossing below the table to the mantelpiece, placing the clubs below the fire and picking up a pipe*) I'm not going to buy new ones. Fact is, I'm giving up golf for good. I'm resigning from the club at the end of the year.
RUTH. But Philip—I don't understand.
PHILIP (*moving slowly to the upstage end of the sofa and sitting*) It's

one of the things I can go without. I'm getting on for sixty—my handicap's gone back to eighteen and sometimes I don't play for a month on end—when the weather's bad. And they're putting up the club subscription on the first of January.

RUTH. Brutes!

PHILIP. Oh, I don't know! (*He begins to fill his pipe*) Everything's getting more expensive—grass seed, chemical dressings, labour—it's no good, Ruth. We've got to draw in our horns. The only thing that seems to remain on the level these days is my income.

RUTH (*wistfully*) Of course, there's the car . . .

PHILIP. The car's a different matter. The car gives everyone pleasure—you, Carol—Denis—I see it isn't in the garage now. I suppose Denis took it.

JACKY. He's gone to see Eric Tranter.

PHILIP. Has he? *That* fellow, eh?

RUTH. But, Philip. I still feel . . .

PHILIP. No, my dear. It's all settled. I've sent in my resignation. (*He lights his pipe*)

RUTH. It seems very unfair.

GRANDMA (*putting her cup on the table at his right*) Especially when you can waste money in sending a chit of a girl to the bioscope three times a week!

JACKY (*jumping up*) And have to keep a nasty old woman in the house who does nothing but grumble and steal buns.

GRANDMA (*rising*) What!

PHILIP. Jacky! How dare you!

JACKY (*bursting into tears*) I'm sorry, Uncle Philip. I'm sorry, but—oh, you don't understand!

(JACKY *rushes from the room*)

GRANDMA (*furious*) I've never been so insulted in all my life—nasty old woman, indeed! (*She sits*) That child must leave the house—leave the house this very moment!

PHILIP. Don't be silly, Grandma. There's nowhere for Jacky to go.

GRANDMA. Back to her precious school.

PHILIP. The "precious school" is closed for Christmas for one thing, and for another—well, she didn't mean any harm.

GRANDMA. Didn't mean any harm! Little did I think I'd ever live to hear a son of mine call his mother a nasty old woman.

PHILIP. I didn't!

GRANDMA. You take her part—it's the same thing.

PHILIP. Jacky's only a child and . . .

GRANDMA. Yes, and there's a way to deal with children . . .

PHILIP. And when it comes down to brass tacks, Grandma—well, you started it—nagging about her having been to the pictures.

GRANDMA. Nagging! Oh, I see. (*Becoming self-pitying*) It's clear enough that I'm not wanted here. Perhaps you'd prefer *me* to go? (*She rises slowly*)

PHILIP. I'm not suggesting that anyone should go—

(GRANDMA *sits quickly*)

—but if you insist on forcing an issue it's quite clear. I've undertaken to have Jacky here over Christmas and there's no alternative. *You*, on the other hand, *have* an alternative. I'm not your only son. There's Paul in Wolverhampton, and there's Mabel, too. In fact, the original arrangement was that you should spend four months of the year with each of us.

GRANDMA. That's right, turn me out—your own mother—turn me out!

PHILIP. I'm not turning you out. I'm merely suggesting that perhaps we've been so long together—it's three years since you were last with Paul or Mabel—that we're beginning to get on each other's nerves a little.

GRANDMA. Very well. I quite understand. (*She rises*) I shall go to Paul in the morning. I'll start packing at once. (*She goes to the door*) At once. You understand?

(*Nobody says anything, so* GRANDMA *goes out with dignity*)

RUTH (*rising*) I suppose I'd better go and stop her.
PHILIP. No. Let her alone. She doesn't mean it—worse luck!
RUTH (*crossing above the sofa to the armchair*) After all, Philip, she *is* your own mother, and Jacky *was* very rude.
PHILIP. Of course Jacky was rude, but Grandma's always had it in for her. Plain jealousy. That's all it is.
RUTH. Then you don't think she *will* go?
PHILIP. Not a hope!
RUTH. Of course, I'll make Jacky apologize . . .
PHILIP. I don't think you'll have to make her. If I'm any judge of human nature she'll do it of her own free will.
RUTH (*sitting in the armchair*) Very well, dear. Now—about the golf club . . .
PHILIP. Let's forget it.
RUTH. I suppose we couldn't get rid of Martha?
PHILIP. Rubbish!
RUTH. I could manage all right. Of course, I have to spend *hours* in queues, but Carol would help me.
PHILIP. A fat lot of help Carol would be, and you know it.
RUTH. Of course, there are her classes at the Art School.
PHILIP. To say nothing of young Martin Latham.
RUTH. I do hope something comes of that. Do you think it will?
PHILIP. In time. Martin's not the sort of fellow to be rushed.

RUTH. Oh, I agree! I can't imagine Martin being "rushed"!
(*She rises*)
PHILIP. Or even "rushing", eh?
RUTH (*crossing to the table*) But, then, I suppose dull men always make the best husbands!
PHILIP. Eh?
RUTH. I mean—Carol might do a great deal worse.
PHILIP. Yes, he may be a bit of a boob on the surface, but he's sound enough. I only wish Denis had more of his—reliability.
RUTH. Denis is all right.
PHILIP. Of course he's all right. Only I'd be better pleased if he wasn't so *restless*.
RUTH. That time he spent in the Air Force, dear—all that excitement and travel. And flapping about! More tea?
PHILIP. No, thanks.
RUTH. Then I'll tell Martha to keep the kettle on. She'll have to make fresh for Carol.

(RUTH *goes out up* L. PHILIP *rises, moves to the mantelpiece and relights his pipe. He hums a few tuneless notes and then picks out a putter from the bag below the fireplace. He plays a few shots at an imaginary ball. Then he remembers, sighs, shakes his head and replaces the club. The telephone bell rings and he crosses to the desk and lifts the receiver*)

PHILIP. Hello! Yes, Caterham six-seven-six . . . Denis? . . . No? This is Mr Stafford speaking . . . No, he's not in. Might be here any moment . . . Certainly, I'll take a message. Who's speaking? (*With a change of manner*) Yes, yes . . . Ring you when he comes in? Very well, I'll tell him . . . Yes, I've got the name *quite* right. Eric Tranter . . . Yes . . . The number? Oh, he knows it? All right . . . 'Bye. (*He replaces the receiver and crosses back to the fireplace. It is obvious that he is a little worried. He picks up a paper from the stool down* R *and sits on the sofa*)

(*After a pause the door opens and* JACKY *looks into the room. She closes the door, crosses and stands with her back to the fire, looking at Philip. She appears dejected.* PHILIP *goes on reading*)

JACKY (*in a small voice*) It's me!
PHILIP (*looking up*) Eh?
JACKY. I said "It's me"!
PHILIP. So I observe. (*He goes on reading*)
JACKY (*after a pause*) Of course, I'm sorry.
PHILIP. Naturally.
JACKY. And I apologize.
PHILIP. No need to apologize to *me*, Jacky.
JACKY. Well, it's your house!
PHILIP. I sometimes wonder.
JACKY. I suppose I shall have to apologize to Grandma, too?

PHILIP. What do *you* think?
JACKY (*gloomily*) I *have* thought.
PHILIP. Good!
JACKY. How she'll gloat. (*She pauses*) Uncle Philip!
PHILIP. Yes?
JACKY. It's awfully difficult apologizing to Grandma.
PHILIP. You ought to know.
JACKY (*kneeling at his feet*) I think she's jealous because I shall be here with you after she's gone—(*she adds*) I hope.
PHILIP. I hope so, too, Jacky.
JACKY. D'you know, if I was old and *she* was young, *I* shouldn't be jealous.
PHILIP. No?
JACKY. No. I should try to be kind to young people—like you are. If she went away there might be room for me—always. I wish I had a home of my own like other girls. I mean a home in England—*here*.
PHILIP. Well, you have. (*He puts a hand on hers*) You're here now, aren't you?
JACKY. Only as a visitor.
PHILIP (*slightly amused*) So you consider yourself a visitor, do you?
JACKY. Oh, I know I don't behave like one—often. But that's what I am—a poor relation—a hanger-on like Grandma. Only she's always here and she ticks off each day of my holidays and stays on here after I'm sent back to school. That's why I try to score off her.
PHILIP. Do you think you *do* score off her? It can't be much fun scoring off people if, after you've scored, you have to come back and crawl.
JACKY. I wonder why I come back and crawl? She wouldn't come back and crawl to me.
PHILIP. Grandma's never been very good at crawling. (*He puts his arm around her shoulders*) Jacky, you're a very decent kid—although you try very hard not to be.
JACKY. I'm not decent, really. I'd like to poison Grandma!
PHILIP (*removing his arm*) Not really?
JACKY. Oh yes, I would. Like they poisoned the beastly old woman in *Death's Sting*.
PHILIP. You won't try, I hope?
JACKY. No. You wouldn't like it, would you?
PHILIP. I shouldn't count on me as an accomplice.
JACKY. Still, I don't think Grandma *ought* to dislike me so.
PHILIP. Even though you want to poison her?
JACKY. But she doesn't know that.
PHILIP. Perhaps she guesses. She's rather good at guessing.
JACKY. She hasn't guessed about the football pool.
PHILIP (*startled*) Football pool? Which football pool?

JACKY. The one you go in for every week with Carol and Denis.

PHILIP. How did *you* know about that?

JACKY. Carol gives them to me to post sometimes.

PHILIP. She would! (*He sighs*) Never trust a woman with a secret.

JACKY. You can trust me, Uncle Philip. I won't betray you. But there'd be an awful "to-do" if Grandma found out, wouldn't there?

PHILIP. You're telling me!

JACKY. Of course, I don't *really* hate her.

PHILIP. And you'd only poison her in—shall we say—a friendly way?

JACKY (*rising and turning to the fire*) I wish she'd come down and I could get it over—the crawling, I mean.

PHILIP. Why not make a *thorough* job of it and go up to her room and apologize there?

JACKY (*gloomily*) It's an idea.

PHILIP. Not a bad one either. You could offer to help her with her unpacking.

JACKY. Unpacking? What's she unpacking?

PHILIP. Her luggage. She went up to pack twenty minutes ago, so by now she'll be *un*packing again.

JACKY. All right. (*She crosses up* L *towards the door*)

PHILIP. Jacky!

JACKY (*turning*) Yes?

PHILIP. Give us a kiss before you go.

JACKY (*coming to the back of the sofa and throwing her arms around his neck*) Oh, Uncle Philip, I do love you so!

PHILIP. Good. But don't tell your aunt. I can't put up with another jealous woman in the house.

JACKY. All right, I won't. It's a secret—like the football pools.

(JACKY *breaks away and runs up* L *to the door. As she reaches it,* RUTH *opens it and enters*)

RUTH. Hello, Jacky.

JACKY. Hello, Aunt Ruth. I'm sorry about—just now.

RUTH (*crossing* C *in front of Jacky*) Never mind, dear.

JACKY. I'm just going up to apologize to Grandma. (*She turns in the doorway*) Damn her eyes!

(JACKY *goes out and bangs the door*)

RUTH (*horrified*) Philip! Did you hear that? (*She crosses to the fireplace with some logs*)

PHILIP. Yes, dear. Never mind. You must often have thought the same.

RUTH (*kneeling in front of the fire*) Philip, I'm worried.

PHILIP. Now what?

ACT I   EASY MONEY

RUTH. About Martin—Martin Latham.

PHILIP. Goodness gracious! Haven't we enough to worry about with our own family without worrying about the people next door?

RUTH (*rising*) But—Martin—it's different.

PHILIP. Out with it then.

RUTH. I don't know really if I ought to tell you. In a way I've been spying.

PHILIP (*surprised*) Spying?

RUTH. I went out to the shed just now to get some logs. You know Martin won't go into the garden after dark since Colonel Rawlings has had that new Alsatian—and the lights were on next door, and the blinds hadn't been drawn. I didn't mean to be curious but I couldn't help seeing.

PHILIP. Seeing what?

RUTH. Martin Latham. (*She sits in the armchair*) He was in that little room at the back all by himself sitting in front of the fire.

PHILIP. Why shouldn't he sit in front of the fire?

RUTH. Philip—it was the *way* he was sitting—with his head in his arms, like this. (*She demonstrates*)

PHILIP. Perhaps he had a headache.

RUTH. That's what I thought at first. (*She rises*) But then, quite suddenly he got up and began to walk about the room, waving his arms. (*She demonstrates*) Then—— (*She hesitates*)

PHILIP. Yes?

RUTH (*sitting quickly*) He sat down again. He looked the picture of misery. I'm afraid he's in some awful trouble.

PHILIP. If he is he won't thank you for interfering.

RUTH. I wasn't going to. But suppose it's to do with Carol?

PHILIP. Why should it be?

RUTH. She's so late. I thought perhaps they were together. Do you think they've had a quarrel?

PHILIP. May have done.

RUTH. Oh, dear!

PHILIP. Why not? A little quarrelling is only healthy before an engagement. It's after one's married it matters.

RUTH. We never quarrelled before *we* were engaged.

PHILIP. Didn't we? You threw a tennis racquet at me, once.

RUTH. Did I?

PHILIP. And hit me!

RUTH. I'd forgotten.

PHILIP (*rubbing his head, thoughtfully*) I haven't.

RUTH. Do you think I ought to tell Carol what I saw?

PHILIP. No. If Martin's quarrelled with her she knows already, and if he's only shaping up for it she'll find out for herself.

(*There is the sound of a door-slam off*)

RUTH (*jumping up and moving* C *above the table*) Here is Carol.

PHILIP. Or Denis!
RUTH. No, dear. Carol only *slams* the door. Denis kicks it shut. It sounds quite different.
PHILIP. Talking about Denis, that fellow Tranter rang up just now. Wants Denis to ring him when he gets back. I've a jolly good mind not to give him the message.
RUTH. Denis would be bound to find out.
PHILIP (*gloomily*) I suppose so.

(CAROL STAFFORD *enters. She is a pretty girl of twenty-two. She has been playing hockey and is dressed accordingly. She looks tired and depressed*)

RUTH. Hello, darling. Here you are at last.
CAROL. Am I late? (*She crosses to* RC) Hello, Father!
RUTH. It doesn't matter, dear. I'll tell Martha and she'll bring fresh tea. (*She moves up* L *towards the door*) Would you like an egg? There's still one left.
CAROL. No, thanks, Mother. I don't want any tea.
RUTH. Aren't you well?
CAROL (*crossing to the fire*) No. I—I've had tea. In Godstone.
RUTH. We've been keeping things for you. I wish you'd rung up and said.
CAROL (*obviously distrait*) Sorry. I forgot.
RUTH. You're sure you wouldn't like another cup now?
CAROL. No thanks. (*She lights a cigarette*)
PHILIP. Good game?
CAROL (*absently*) Eh? Oh, yes.
PHILIP. Who won?
CAROL. We did. Four—one, or five—one, I forget.

(RUTH *and* PHILIP *exchange glances*)

RUTH. Well, it was a nice afternoon for it.
CAROL. Yes. Wasn't it.
PHILIP. Score any goals yourself?
CAROL. Two.
PHILIP. That's splendid. You'll get into that county side yet.
CAROL (*indifferently*) I may. In fact—I am. Some of the selectors were there this afternoon. I'm to play against Hampshire. (*She sits on the stool down* R)
PHILIP. Splendid! Congratulations, Carol.
CAROL. Thanks.
RUTH. You don't seem very pleased about it, dear.
CAROL. Of course I'm pleased.
RUTH (*moving behind the sofa; anxiously*) You haven't been hurt, have you?
CAROL. Hurt?
RUTH. Struck by the ball, I mean—nasty hard thing! I can never understand why you don't play with a soft one.

CAROL. Don't be silly, Mother dear.
PHILIP. Well, you don't seem quite yourself, old thing.
CAROL. I'm tired, that's all.
PHILIP. Then I should have a good rest.
RUTH. I expect Martin is excited by the news, isn't he, dear?
CAROL. Why should he be excited? Anyway, he doesn't know yet.
RUTH. But I thought he was coming to watch your match. He always does.
CAROL. He didn't today. I—I expect something must have detained him.
RUTH. What a pity. Especially as you scored two goals.
CAROL (*peeved*) For goodness' sake, Mother, can't we talk about something else besides hockey? (*She rises and moves up to the fire*)
RUTH. I was, dear. I was talking about Martin.
CAROL (*now angry*) Well, about Martin, then!
RUTH. Very well, dear. I understand. It's only natural you should be upset if he didn't come to watch you play.
CAROL (*frantic*) I'm *not* upset. (*She snatches up a paper and crosses to the other side of the room*) Do please leave me alone! (*She sits at the desk*)
RUTH. But, dear . . . (*She catches* PHILIP'*s eye*) Of course.

(*There are two heavy thuds off*)

Ah! Here's Denis at last. I'll clear up the tea things. (*She moves to the table and starts to clear it*)

(DENIS STAFFORD *enters up* L. *He is a goodish-looking young man, fairly robust and decisive in his manners. He is twenty-seven, but four years in the Forces make him appear older than his years. He wears what appears to be his demob. suit*)

Hello, Denis. Here you are then! (*She kisses him*)
DENIS. Hello, Mother. Any tea left?
RUTH. But I thought you *had* your tea?
DENIS (*putting his arm around her shoulders*) Whatever made you think that?
RUTH. Martha said you'd rung up and said you were staying out.
DENIS. Oh, lord! So I did! I changed my mind. Sorry!
RUTH (*picking up the teapot and waving it about*) Really, this is a very difficult household to run. Carol says she *will* be in to tea and stays out, and *you* say you won't be in to tea and come in.
DENIS. It doesn't matter. I can easily go without.
RUTH. Of course not, dear, it's only . . .
PHILIP. I really can't see any reason why Denis shouldn't have the tea that's been kept for Carol.
RUTH. No, I suppose not. I never thought of that. I'll tell

MARTHA. (*She goes to the door up* L) Thank you, Philip. You're very helpful—sometimes.

(RUTH *goes.* DENIS *crosses to the fire and bends to warm his hands*)

PHILIP. Cold out?

DENIS. Getting a bit chilly. We'll have a frost, probably. Good game?

PHILIP. Only average. Thought I'd get a birdie at the fifteenth, but my approach went over the green and into the brook.

DENIS. Bad luck!

PHILIP. There's wonderful news about Carol, though.

DENIS. Eh? (*He straightens up from the fire*) What? I say, has old Martin spoken up like a man at last? Well, I'm damned! (*He crosses below the table towards Carol*)

CAROL (*icily*) Try not to be a bigger fool than God made you, Denis.

DENIS. Sorry! (*He looks enquiringly at Philip*)

PHILIP. She's been picked for the county against Hampshire.

DENIS. I say! Fine show! Good old Carol!

CAROL. Thank you.

DENIS. That ought to stir up old stick-in-the-mud a bit! By the way, where is he?

CAROL. Who?

DENIS. Martin, of course.

CAROL. I haven't the slightest idea.

DENIS. I want to see him about something—rather important. I thought he would come back with you.

PHILIP (*seeing that Carol doesn't intend to reply*) He didn't go to the match.

DENIS. Hello! The course of true love running off the tarmac, eh?

CAROL (*rising*) I've already asked you not to be a fool, Denis. (*She moves up to the bookcase* C *and looks at some books*)

DENIS. Oh! So it's *serious*?

PHILIP (*intervening*) Oh, by the way, Denis, there was a phone call for you. That fellow—what's-his-name—Tranter.

DENIS. Eric? Oh, perhaps that explains. (*He hurries to the telephone and lifts the receiver*) Long Acre four-three-one-nine. Hope I haven't missed him again!

PHILIP (*fencing*) I don't suppose it's anything very important.

DENIS (*evasively*) No, of course not. (*Into the telephone*) Hello! Is that you, Eric? Denis here . . . I've only just got back . . . Oh, you *were*? . . . I see . . . Yes . . . Yes . . . Here, I say! That's a bit awkward, isn't it? . . . I didn't realize the thing had to be fixed up so soon as this . . . Yes, yes. I understand that part, but . . . I haven't had much time to move yet, have I? . . . Of course, I'm not backing out—no, *really*, old boy, I'm not, but this is shorter notice than I expected . . . I'll see what I can do . . . Tell you what, I'll ring you back again later tonight . . . Oh, you won't? First thing in the morning then . . . Yes, for certain . . . Yes. Cheerio. (*He replaces the receiver*)

(RUTH *enters up* L *with the teapot*)

RUTH. Here you are, dear. Would you like an egg? There's one left. (*She crosses to* C *above the table*)

DENIS (*obviously preoccupied*) No, thanks, Mother. As a matter of fact, I don't think I want anything.

RUTH. But, Denis—just now you said . . .

DENIS. Did I? (*Remembering*) Oh, yes! So I did. Sorry! (*He moves in and sits* L *of the table*)

RUTH. And you'd like the egg?

DENIS. No, I'll just have a cup of tea.

RUTH. Very well, dear. I'll tell Martha or she may boil it.

DENIS. Boil what?

RUTH. The egg!

(RUTH *goes out up* L. DENIS *pours himself some tea. There is a pause. He shapes to speak to Philip and hesitates. There is another pause*)

DENIS. Are you going out later, Carol?

CAROL. Not that I know of. Why? (*She takes a book from the bookcase, crosses to the desk, and sits down*)

DENIS. Just wondered, that's all.

(CAROL *reads. There is another pause and then* DENIS *rises and crosses, with his tea, to the fire. He stands by the fireplace*)

I say! Dad!

PHILIP (*looking up*) Yes, old man?

DENIS. I—(*he hesitates*) I don't suppose you could lend me five hundred pounds?

PHILIP. Five hundred pounds! Good heavens!

DENIS. Three-fifty, then?

PHILIP. Not a hope, old son. As a matter of fact, I've been working out a scheme for cutting down expenses all round. The cost of living these days seems to go up and up and . . . (*Suddenly*) You haven't been getting yourself into some mess, have you?

DENIS (*laughing*) Good lord, no.

PHILIP. You'd tell me if you have?

DENIS. Of course I would. (*Serious again*) No, it's nothing like that—quite the reverse in fact. I've had a chance to get in on something pretty wizard, but the trouble is that I need five hundred or I'm a non-starter. I've got a hundred and fifty but that's not enough.

PHILIP. A hundred and fifty?

(DENIS *nods*)

Oh yes, the money your godfather left you. (*He is rather worried*) I say, old son, what *is* this scheme?

DENIS. It's a bit complicated—would take too long to explain.

PHILIP. I suppose your friend, Tranter, has something to do with it?

DENIS. Yes. (*He pauses*) Why?

PHILIP. Then, if you'll take my advice, I'd keep out of it.

DENIS (*puzzled*) I say, Dad! Why have you always got it in so for poor old Eric?

PHILIP (*defensively*) Have I?

DENIS. Of course. I've only to mention his name and you go all bleak.

PHILIP. Well—I—I suppose he's not the sort of fellow I'd trust.

DENIS. For what reason, Dad? You must have a reason!

PHILIP. Nothing *concrete*—no!

DENIS. That's a bit unfair, isn't it?

PHILIP. Perhaps so, perhaps not. You'll go careful, old son, won't you?

DENIS. Trust me! I'm out of my rompers, you know!

(*They laugh.* JACKY *opens the door up* L. GRANDMA *enters.* JACKY *follows her in.* GRANDMA *seems to have completely recovered her spirits, but* JACKY *looks glum*)

GRANDMA (*coming* C) Ha! Everybody home! That's right. There's nothing I like better than a happy family circle. (*With a meaning look at Jacky*) Although sometimes it's larger than is convenient.

(*But for once* JACKY *refuses to bite*)

I hope you're not overtired, Carol dear?

CAROL. No, thank you.

PHILIP. She's picked for the county next week.

GRANDMA. *Picking* what? (*She crosses to the armchair and sits*)

JACKY (*delighted*) I say! What scrumptious news! (*She rushes at Carol*) Gee! I'll come and watch! The flicks can go hell one Saturday!

CAROL. Oh, don't, Jacky!

JACKY (*surprised and abashed*) Sorry, what's up? (*She breaks* LC)

DENIS. It's all right, Jacky. Love's young dream and all that. You're too young to understand. Boy friend cut the match date, that's all.

JACKY. Didn't Martin come to the game?

CAROL. I really can't see what business it is of everybody.

GRANDMA. Perhaps Mr Right doesn't approve of young women rushing about in short skirts with sticks. Now when *I* was a girl . . .

JACKY. When *you* were a girl . . .

PHILIP (*warningly*) Jacky!

JACKY. I'm sure things were quite different. (*She sits* R *of the table*)

GRANDMA. The Mr Right of those days expected young women to be womanly.

JACKY (*in a low voice*) And old cats to be catty!

GRANDMA (*dangerously*) What's that?

JACKY. Nothing. I was only thinking.

DENIS. Talking of Mr Rights, just slip next door, Jacky, and see if Martin Latham is about. If so, ask him to come in.

(JACKY *rises*)

Tell him Carol wants to see him.

CAROL (*rising*) I don't!

DENIS. Well, I do. It's the same thing.

CAROL. No, it isn't!

DENIS (*to Jacky*) Tell him *I* want to see him, then.

JACKY. Oke!

(JACKY *hurries out up* L)

CAROL. If you want to see Martin, why not go yourself? Why ask him in here?

DENIS. I'm expecting another phone call, for one thing, and it gives you a chance to make it up.

CAROL. Make *what* up?

DENIS. Whatever it is you've bust up about.

CAROL. Look here—how dare you . . .?

(RUTH *enters up* L)

RUTH. Jacky, dear—where is she?

DENIS. Gone next door to fetch Martin.

RUTH (*looking at Carol*) Why?

DENIS. Because I want to see him.

(CAROL *crosses to the window*)

RUTH. Will he be expecting tea? (*She moves above the table*)

DENIS. I shouldn't think so.

RUTH. In that case he probably will. I'd better tell Martha.

(RUTH *goes towards the door up* L, *but as she reaches it*, JACKY *enters*)

JACKY. Here he is!

(MARTIN LATHAM *enters. He is a robust, rather stocky young man of twenty-eight. He has a resolute and forthright manner and is much addicted to tweeds, caps, pipes and mackintoshes. In short, he might be described as being part of the backbone of the British nation*)

MARTIN (*coming* L *of the table; in a deep sepulchral voice*) Oh, hello!

(JACKY *drops down* L *and kneels on the chair by the desk*)

RUTH. Good evening, Martin. Come in.
MARTIN. Thank you.
RUTH. Have you had tea?
MARTIN. No.
RUTH. There you are. I knew it. (*She makes a move as though to go to the door up* L)
MARTIN (*stopping her*) But I don't want any, thank you, Mrs Stafford.
RUTH. You're sure? (*She crosses down* R *and sits on the stool*)
MARTIN. Quite. Good evening, Denis. (*He sees Carol*) Oh, you're—you're back, then?
CAROL. Yes.
PHILIP. She's been picked for the county.
MARTIN (*still gloomy*) I say. That's good, isn't it?
RUTH. We thought you'd be excited.
JACKY (*jumping up and running to Martin*) Can I come with you to watch the match?
MARTIN (*moving away from her a little, below the table*) Well—I—I—er—might not be able to go.
GRANDMA. What did I tell you?
MARTIN (*noticing her*) Oh, good evening!
GRANDMA. Now, when I was a girl, any self-respecting Mr Right . . .
PHILIP (*intervening*) Yes, Grandma, yes!

(JACKY *returns to the desk chair*)

MARTIN (*to Denis*) You want to see me?
DENIS (*crossing below the settee to join Martin*) Yes. I would have come in only there may be a phone call. We can slip up to my room, though, and have a chat. (*He moves to take Martin's arm*)
MARTIN. Is it about that—*other matter*?
DENIS. Of course.
MARTIN. Oh, I see.
DENIS. You said you'd think it over.
MARTIN. Yes.
DENIS. Well, have you?
MARTIN. No.
DENIS. Right. We'll think it over together. (*He tries to urge Martin towards the door*)
MARTIN (*resisting*) I don't think it would be much good. I'm sorry. I ought to have told you from the outset that it's not the sort of thing I'd care to be associated with.
DENIS. Here, I say!
MARTIN. I'm not saying there's anything *wrong* with it, of course, but . . .
DENIS. You'd rather be included out of it—is that what you mean?

MARTIN. Exactly! Sorry!

DENIS. Well, I know where I am, at any rate. The only hope now is to win the football pool. (*He moves up* R *of the table*)

GRANDMA. Football pool!

PHILIP (*laughing uneasily*) No! No! Denis is just joking.

DENIS (*turning*) No, I'm not joking. I want to raise five hundred pounds and it looks as if the best chance is the football pool.

GRANDMA. Am I to understand that my wishes as regards gambling have been disregarded?

(MARTIN *sits* L *of the table*)

DENIS (*moving to the back of the sofa*) I don't know about gambling, but Dad, Carol and I certainly have a flutter on the penny points.

PHILIP. Really, Denis—I . . .

DENIS. And I'm sick of all this secrecy about it. (*To Grandma*) We send in seven-and-sixpence worth—half a crown apiece—each week.

GRANDMA (*in fury*) Little did I think I should find myself in a house of sin!

JACKY (*lightly*) Especially at your age!

GRANDMA (*sweeping on*) Little did I think that my own family would prove to be wanton gamblers and dice players . . .

RUTH. Really, Grandma—I really think . . .

GRANDMA (*rising*) Be silent! (*With great dignity*) I shall not remain under this roof a day longer. (*She crosses above the sofa to* C) There is a doom on this house, the doom that follows the curse of gambling as surely as the night follows the day. I shall not remain here to see it. Philip! Tomorrow morning I shall be leaving here for Wolverhampton. Kindly look up the right trains and telegraph Paul to meet me at the station. Now I am going to pack. (*She moves towards the door up* L)

JACKY (*rising and running to join Grandma*) May I help you?

GRANDMA. No, you may *not*.

(GRANDMA *goes out with great dignity. There is a pause*)

CAROL. It looks as if you've done it now, Denis! (*She crosses to the chair at the desk*)

RUTH (*to Philip*) Do you think she means it?

PHILIP (*soberly*) D'you know, I believe she *does*, this time.

JACKY (*crossing to the sofa*) I wish she'd let me help her. Once she'd packed I'd lose the keys and then she couldn't unpack again. (*She sits on the lower end of the sofa*)

RUTH (*reproving*) Jacky!

JACKY. Sorry! But I can't be a hypocrite, Aunt Ruth.

PHILIP. Denis, I think you might have been more careful . . .

DENIS. I really don't see why you should all treat me as if I'd committed murder. You *want* the old girl to clear out—you've

been wanting it for years—and if I've fixed it for you you ought to be grateful.
RUTH. Denis! Really. Don't forget we've a visitor. (*She indicates Martin*)
DENIS. I don't count Martin as a visitor.

(MARTIN *smiles sadly*)

The sooner he gets to know all the worse side of the family the better. Eh, Carol?
CAROL (*rising*) Denis. As I've already told you—you're a fool.

(CAROL *moves to the door up* L *and goes out.* MARTIN *rises, follows her up to the door and hesitates—and the door closes*)

RUTH. Philip, if Grandma really is serious, hadn't you better ring up Paul as she said?
PHILIP. Plenty of time for that later on when the cheap rates come on. Hello! Six o'clock. (*He rises*) Anybody want to hear the news?
RUTH. No, I don't think so, dear.
PHILIP (*crossing towards the door down* L) In that case, Denis, just switch it through to the other room, would you?

(PHILIP *goes out down* L)

DENIS. Well, having successfully put the cat among the pigeons —or vice versa—I think I'll have a stroll. (*He moves up to the radio and switches it on*)
RUTH. But, dear—you said you were expecting another phone call.
DENIS (*looking at Martin*) I don't think it matters much, now.
MARTIN. I'm sorry if you feel I've let you down.
DENIS. No, of course not. That's all right, pal! (*He goes up* L *to the door*) So long!
RUTH. You won't be late for supper, will you?
DENIS. No. I'll be back soon. I only want to think.

(DENIS *goes out*)

MARTIN (*moving to the back of the sofa, downstage end*) Well, Mrs Stafford, I must be moving on, too.
JACKY. No, don't go yet. I want to talk to you.
MARTIN. What about?
JACKY. Something important—very, very important.
RUTH (*rising*) Important! (*She moves up between the sofa and the table*) That reminds me. I had something very important to do. Now what was it? Ah, I know—the egg!

(RUTH *crosses to the door up* L *and goes out*)

MARTIN. Well, what is it, Jacky?
JACKY (*jumping up*) Sit down!

MARTIN (*moving away below the chair* R *of the table*) Look here, I hope what you want to say won't take long. I've——
JACKY. Siddown, you! (*She pushes him into the chair* R *of the table*)
MARTIN (*sitting*) Oh!
JACKY. And you stay parked there till I've said my piece. Get that, big boy?
MARTIN. I've really no time this evening for fooling . . .
JACKY. Who's fooling? Do you know what Grandma calls you?
MARTIN. I had no idea Mrs Stafford Senior called me anything.
JACKY. She calls you "Mr Right".
MARTIN (*puzzled*) Mr Right?
JACKY. Yes. But I can't see much right about you.
MARTIN. But I don't understand. Why should Mrs Stafford call me Mr Right?
JACKY. She thinks you're Carol's "Mr Right".
MARTIN (*with a change of manner, and very gloomy*) Oh, I see!
JACKY. What's it all about? This row between you and Carol?
MARTIN. There isn't any row. (*He starts to rise*) And I don't intend . . .
JACKY. Sit down, you! (*She pushes him down again*) You're sure not going to make a get-away from this. Carol's as sick as mud because you didn't go to the hockey game with her. Why didn't you?
MARTIN. Because I—because I had something else to do.
JACKY. Rot! You're as sick as mud, too. Anyone could see that the moment you came in. And why were you walking up and down the road groaning when I found you?
MARTIN (*half rising again*) Once and for all, Jacky, I don't propose . . .
JACKY (*pushing him down again*) That's just it—you don't!
MARTIN. Don't what?
JACKY. Propose. To Carol. I mean, you're in love with her, aren't you?
MARTIN. Really, I . . .
JACKY. Are you in love with Carol, or aren't you?
MARTIN. I—I'm very fond of her, certainly.
JACKY. And you want to marry her?
MARTIN. I *did* want to marry her.
JACKY. Then what's changed you?
MARTIN. Nothing's changed me.
JACKY. Then you *still* want to marry her? Hey?
MARTIN. I've been thinking . . .
JACKY. If you're in love, sucker, you're not capable of thinking.
MARTIN. Hey, damn it! What do you know about it?
JACKY. What do I . . .? (*She crosses* L *below the table and turns*) If you went to the flicks more you'd find that even a second feature picture could teach you that! Here you are in love with

Carol and Carol in love with you and nothing done about it because you go on being—sub-tropical! Carol's my cousin and she's been pretty decent to me. I'm not going to stand by and see you make her miserable. Carol wants you to marry her.

MARTIN. Did she say so?

JACKY (*crossing below the table towards the sofa*) No, you dope. Of course not. I can't think *why* she wants to marry you, but she does. I wouldn't marry you if you were the only man alive.

MARTIN. Thank God for that!

JACKY. Come clean, now. Why don't you propose to Carol? Out with it.

MARTIN. I'm damned if I will.

JACKY. You'll feel better if you get it off your chest, and I might be able to help you.

MARTIN. You?

JACKY. Why not?

MARTIN (*after a pause*) Jacky, you're a decent kid—in a way. If I tell you, will you promise me something?

JACKY. Sure thing, boss. (*She sits on the back of the sofa*)

MARTIN. You'll never breathe a word to any living soul?

JACKY (*with an appropriate gesture*) Cut my throat!

MARTIN. All right. (*He rises and begins to walk around the room*) I suppose it's all to do with this National Service.

JACKY. But you've finished with that.

MARTIN (*crossing behind the table and then down* L) I may have finished with it but the results remain. I haven't proposed to Carol because I see no hope of ever being in a position to marry her. I was in the army two years and . . .

JACKY. But you're back in your job.

MARTIN (*crossing up* C) Yes, I'm back to exactly where I was. Two years wasted. Two years that can never be returned.

JACKY. There's a lot more the same as you.

MARTIN (*walking about up* C) Of course there are, but that doesn't make it any better. There are thousands of chaps like me. I wasn't much good in the Forces. I didn't get sent overseas, I didn't get called out during a dock strike. Nothing happened. (*He stops pacing*) I didn't even get recommended for a stripe. I don't suppose I showed enough initiative.

JACKY (*frankly*) No, I don't suppose you did.

MARTIN (*waving his arms and pacing up and down more frantically*) There you are, you see! Two years wasted. A junior accountant in the City and it'll be ten years at least before I get a reasonably good salary. What's the use of asking Carol to marry me?

JACKY. She'd wait.

MARTIN. Why *should* she?

JACKY. Because she's "in lurve".

MARTIN (*coming down* L) No, it wouldn't be right. Carol's used to a comfortable home.

JACKY. See here, mister—I say, I don't suppose you could sit down for a bit, could you? Talking to you is rather like watching a table-tennis match.

MARTIN. Sorry. (*He sits at the desk*)

JACKY. None of this explains why you cut the hockey game.

MARTIN. I didn't want to cut it. It was hell not going to see her play, but I thought it out and came to the conclusion that it wouldn't be honourable. If I can't marry Carol then I shouldn't propose to her, and if I can't propose to her it isn't fair for me to go on being so friendly with her.

JACKY (*rising and crossing to him*) D'you know, mister, you're so blessed heroic you ought to be in glorious technicolor. I'll tell you what you're going to do, and you're going to do it right now—this very night. You're going to ask Carol to marry you.

MARTIN. I'm not!

JACKY. Oh, yes, you are! I'm not going to be done out of being a bridesmaid by a silly twirp like you. You'll ask Carol to marry you and she'll say yes.

MARTIN. But—— (*Suddenly*) D'you know, Jacky, I believe you're right. (*He rises*) By God, I will!

JACKY. Attaboy! (*She shakes his hand*)

MARTIN. I'll ask her tonight.

JACKY. Is that a promise?

MARTIN (*crossing below her towards* R) At least, I think I will.

JACKY (*shouting*) Is that a promise?

MARTIN. Yes. Yes, Jacky. It's a promise.

JACKY (*moving towards the door up* L) Swell! I'll go and fetch her!

MARTIN (*about to follow*) No. No. Don't do that—I . . .

JACKY. Strike while the iron's hot!

(*The door opens and* CAROL *enters*)

No need. Here she is!

CAROL (*coming down* L *of the table*) Hello, Martin, I thought you'd gone.

MARTIN (*very nervously*) No, I haven't gone.

CAROL. You're still here?

MARTIN. Yes—I'm—I'm still here.

(JACKY *crosses above the table and comes down* R *of Martin*)

CAROL. A bit chilly tonight, isn't it?

MARTIN. Yes—yes—it is—decidedly chilly. (*He mops his brow*)

CAROL. Seasonable, though.

MARTIN. Yes. Quite seasonable.

(*There is a pause*)

JACKY (*to Martin*) Get on with it!

MARTIN. I think it would be much better if you went away, Jacky.

JACKY. And I think it would be much better if I didn't.
CAROL. Is anything the matter?
MARTIN. No, no—of course not!
CAROL. I'm glad.
JACKY. Carol, Martin wants to ask you something.
CAROL. Does he? What is it, Martin?
MARTIN. Well—I—well, it's like this . . .

(*The door opens and* RUTH *hurries in*)

RUTH (*coming* C *above the table*) Hello, Martin. I thought you'd gone.
JACKY. Damn!
MARTIN (*moving up* C) I'm just going, Mrs Stafford!
JACKY (*catching him by the coat tails*) Oh, no, you're not!
RUTH. What a good thing nobody had the egg for tea.
CAROL. Why, Mother?
RUTH. Martha dropped it on the kitchen floor just now and it was bad.
JACKY (*crossing to* L *of Ruth*) Shall I come with you and help wipe it up?
RUTH. No, it's all right, Jacky—Martha is coping with it.
JACKY (*dragging* RUTH *towards the window*) Then come with me into the garden and help me cut the lawn.
RUTH. Cut the lawn in the dark in the middle of December? Are you all right, Jacky?
JACKY. Yes, Aunt Ruth, perfectly!
RUTH (*to Carol*) There's nothing going on, is there?
CAROL. Of course not.
RUTH. I thought perhaps Martin was asking you . . .
CAROL (*terrified*) Mother!
RUTH. To go to St Jude's whist drive next Wednesday.
JACKY. There is something going on, Aunt Ruth—isn't there, Martin? And I think it would be better if . . .

(*The door opens and* GRANDMA *enters. She has her sleeves rolled up*)

GRANDMA (*stamping across to the fireplace*) Has anyone seen that book Mrs Maltravers gave me, Ruth? *Charity—the Greatest of Virtues.* I don't intend to leave that behind!
RUTH. Then you really are leaving us?
GRANDMA. Of course I am! Didn't you hear me say so?
RUTH (*moving to the back of the sofa*) Yes, but you've said so before, often.
GRANDMA. Has Philip rung up Paul?
RUTH. Not yet, dear. I think he will later, if you're serious.
JACKY. He's looking up the trains *now*.
GRANDMA. Oh, he is, is he? Very eager to get rid of me, I must say. (*She searches round for the book*) It's a black book with gold lettering.

JACKY (*to Martin*) Why don't you take Carol into the garden?
RUTH. The garden—my dear Jacky, why do you keep on so about the garden?

(DENIS *enters*)

Oh, here you are, Denis—have you had your tea? I hope so, because the egg is bad—oh, yes, of course you have.
JACKY (*crossing to* C) What's brought you back? I thought you were going for a walk.
DENIS. It's started to snow.
RUTH. Has it? Then perhaps we shall have a nice "cardy" Christmas—you know, with robins!

(GRANDMA *sits on the sofa, downstage end*)

DENIS. It's more like sleet, really.

(*The door down* L *is opened hurriedly and* PHILIP *enters. He stands in the doorway holding on to the lintel. He has a piece of paper in his hand. It is evident that something has happened very out of the ordinary*)

RUTH. Philip! What on earth's the matter?
PHILIP. I—I—— (*He is looking rather like a goldfish*)
CAROL. Father!
DENIS (*hurrying down* L) Are you *ill*, Dad?
PHILIP (*still making odd sounds*) I—I—let me—sit down.

(DENIS *helps* PHILIP *into the chair* L *of the table. He stands* L *of* PHILIP. CAROL *stands* L *of Denis*)

Is there any brandy in the house?
RUTH. No, I'm afraid not. Martha had the last of it for the pudding.
PHILIP (*faintly*) Never mind.
RUTH. You're ill, dear. I'll telephone Dr Macaulay at once. (*She hurries to the desk*) What's his number, Carol?

(JACKY *moves above the sofa*)

PHILIP. No. I'm all right. Don't fetch the doctor. I'll be quite all right in a minute.
RUTH (*hurrying back above the table*) Have some water. Oh, dear, there isn't any! Never mind, have a sip of milk. (*She picks up the milk jug*)
PHILIP. For heaven's sake! (*He waves it away*) Do you want me to be sick?
RUTH. No, dear—certainly not!
DENIS. What is it, Dad? Are you sure we hadn't better phone Macaulay?
PHILIP. Quite sure, Denis. Quite sure, Denis. I'm better now. Felt a bit faint, that was all. The fact is I've had rather a shock.
CAROL. A shock, father?

PHILIP. No end of a shock. And, come to think of it, it's going to be a bit of a shock to you, too.

DENIS. Well?

PHILIP. Well—(*he pauses*) I know it seems utterly ridiculous, but—but the football pool's come up!

DENIS
JACKY } (*together*) What!
CAROL

RUTH. The football pool, Philip?

PHILIP. Yes. Sounds silly, I admit, but it's come up—the penny points!

DENIS. Dad, you're not fooling?

PHILIP. Of course I'm not fooling. D'you think I'd feel as ill as this if I was fooling?

CAROL. You're quite sure?

PHILIP. Yes. I don't think I've made any mistake. I heard the results coming through on the wireless and jotted them down—the same as I always do—then when I came to check it over with the coupon I found we had a column all correct. Then I felt faint.

DENIS. Let me see it.

(PHILIP *hands him the coupon copy*)

One, two, two, draw . . . (*He continues to check it over*) By God, it *seems* all right!

MARTIN (*coming down* C, R *of the table*) Excuse me, but I suppose that's a correct copy of the coupon sent in?

DENIS. Yes. We always check it over—all three of us.

PHILIP. Of course, I may not have put down the results right—from the wireless, I mean. I had no idea—of course—that . . . (*He dries up*)

CAROL. The only thing we can do is to wait for a paper.

JACKY. And they won't be here for another hour.

CAROL. An hour! I can't bear it!

MARTIN. There's no need for that if you will allow me to use the phone.

RUTH. Of course, Martin. But why?

MARTIN. I've a friend on the editorial staff of the *Standard*. The paper is out in London by now. He'll know.

CAROL. Oh, yes, Martin. Do. Hurry! Hurry!

(*They all propel* MARTIN *over to the desk. He picks up the receiver*)

DENIS. By gosh, Dad! If we *have* won it!

RUTH. I'm sure we haven't, Denis. It's bound to be a mistake!

MARTIN (*into the telephone*) Exchange? Get me Central three thousand, will you . . . Yes, Central three thousand.

DENIS. Why should it be a mistake, Mother? *Somebody's* bound to win it—why not us?

RUTH. Because—because we are—us.

MARTIN (*into the telephone*) Central three thousand? . . . Can you put me on to Mr Rodney, please?
GRANDMA. Well, all I can say is . . .
JACKY (*pointing to the telephone*) Sshh!
GRANDMA. What?
JACKY. Sshh!
MARTIN (*into the telephone*) Hello. Is that you, Henry? . . . Latham here . . . Martin Latham. Sorry to bother you, old man, but some friends of mine here in Caterham seem to think they've won a football pool . . . Yes, heard it on the wireless and want to check over the results. Have you a copy of your sports edition handy? . . . Oh? . . . Oh, yes. (*He turns to the others*) Which firm is it?
DENIS. Imperials.
MARTIN (*into the telephone*) Imperials . . . (*To the others*) Treble chance or points?
PHILIP. We've stuck to points!
MARTIN (*into the telephone*) Points . . . Oh, yes, of course, you tabulate them, don't you? Hold on while I get pencil and paper.

(CAROL *rushes to the desk and hands him a sheet of paper.* MARTIN *produces a pencil. He sits at the desk*)

Right-ho, fire away . . . One, two, two, x, x, one, two, x, one, one, two, one, x, two, one, one. Yes, I've got that . . . Thanks, Harry. Good-bye. (*He puts down the receiver, rises and hands the piece of paper to Denis*) Here you are.
DENIS (*checking over the pool copy*) One, two, two . . . x, two . . . (*Very quietly*) There's no doubt about it—Dad's right—we've won it!
JACKY. Yippee!
RUTH. Will it be much?
DENIS. Several thousands, for certain.
RUTH. Several thousand?
DENIS (*moving to Ruth above the table*) The lowest first dividend paid by Imperials this season is two thousand, eight hundred odd. It's a sixteen-match pool, remember. I don't see any reason why it should be less than that—might easily be *twenty* thousand.
PHILIP. Well, even if it's as much as the lowest it will be worth having. Nearly three thousand pounds. A thousand apiece. Not bad, eh, Carol?
MARTIN. Excuse me, is Carol in this, too?
PHILIP. Of course she is. We've been in partnership—all three of us—Carol and Denis and I.
MARTIN. Then Carol has a third share?
PHILIP. Most certainly she has. You don't think we're going to try and crook her, do you?
MARTIN (*with sudden gloom*) Oh! Oh, I see! (*He crosses above the table and stands by the armchair*)

GRANDMA (*rising and crossing to* R *of the table*) Am I to understand that between you you may have won so much as twenty thousand pounds?

DENIS. More, perhaps, Grandma.

GRANDMA. Perhaps I've been a little harsh in my judgement of you.

PHILIP. Eh?

GRANDMA. Of course, gambling is a deadly sin, but . . .

JACKY. Not when you win, eh?

GRANDMA (*ignoring this*) But, of course, football is not like horses or cards or greyhounds, is it?

PHILIP. It's the same principle, Grandma.

GRANDMA. Perhaps so, perhaps not! However, just this once I feel I should be justified in overlooking the matter. You needn't bother to ring Paul, Philip. I forgive you. (*She sits* L *of the table*)

PHILIP. Well, I'm damned.

(*For a moment there is silence*)

DENIS. Let's see. We have to make a claim, don't we? First by telegram, and then by registered letter.

PHILIP. Yes, old son. We won't forget that part, will we?

RUTH (*suddenly*) I've just thought of something.

PHILIP. What?

RUTH. I suppose you *posted* it?

DENIS. Posted what, Mother?

RUTH. Why, the coupon, of course! You know how careless people are in this house. There was that cheque to Conways. It was on the sideboard for weeks, and he wrote *such* a rude letter . . .

DENIS (*laughing*) *Of course* the coupon was posted. Eh, Dad?

PHILIP (*laughing also*) Of course.

DENIS. You posted it yourself, didn't you?

PHILIP. No.

DENIS. What!

PHILIP. I gave it to Carol.

DENIS (*crossing to Carol*) Then *you* did, Carol?

CAROL. No. I gave it to Jacky.

DENIS. To Jacky! (*Moving towards Jacky*) Then *you* posted it, Jacky?

JACKY Yes.

DENIS. You're quite sure?

JACKY. Dead certain.

CAROL. It's all right. As a matter of fact, I saw Jacky post it myself. We were going into Caterham on Wednesday night. She had several letters to post, so I gave her the football pool to post with them. I saw her cross the road at the top of Church Hill and put them in the box.

PHILIP (*gaily*) Everything's all right, then?

JACKY. Of course everything's all right. You don't think I'd be such a juggins as to forget to post it?
PHILIP. Of course not, Jacky! Sorry!
GRANDMA. Nothing that girl did or didn't do would surprise me! (*She rises and moves up* L *towards the door*) Well, I'll just go and finish my unpacking.

(GRANDMA *goes out*)

RUTH (*after a pause*) It's almost a pity that Grandma didn't find out until—until——(*She hesitates*)
PHILIP. Until she'd gone off to Paul, eh?
RUTH. Well, in a way—yes! But I suppose there's always something.
PHILIP (*rising to* LC) You know, this deserves a celebration of some sort. I suggest that we go down to the Valley and see if we can raise a bottle of champagne from somewhere. (*He moves up stage*) What do you say, Denis?
DENIS. Jolly good idea, Dad. Come along! (*He crosses in front of Philip to the door up* L)
JACKY. May I come too?
PHILIP. If you like . . .
JACKY. Wait till I get my blazer!

(JACKY *dashes out up* L)

RUTH (*as they move towards the door*) But, Philip, dear, you know that champagne doesn't agree with you. The last time you had champagne . . .

(DENIS *holds the door open*)

PHILIP (*returning a pace or two*) I don't care if it agrees with me or not. I'm going to drink a whole bottle. (*At the door*) Coming, Carol?
CAROL. No, thanks, Father.
PHILIP. All right. (*To Denis*) Come along, old son. (*He turns to Ruth*) If we're not back by eight you'd better send Grandma to bail us out!

(PHILIP *slaps Denis on the back and they go out laughing and talking*)

RUTH (*opening the door and calling after them*) Do be careful, dear. Remember you're a sidesman at St Jude's.

(RUTH *goes out. There is a pause.* CAROL *looks enquiringly at* MARTIN *but he remains silent*)

CAROL. Well, Martin?
MARTIN. I—I suppose I'd better be going.
CAROL. But I thought you had something important to tell me.
MARTIN. Yes, I had, but—but—well, it doesn't matter now.

CAROL. Oh! Shall I be seeing you tomorrow?

MARTIN. No—I shall be rather booked up tomorrow, I'm afraid.

CAROL. I see.

MARTIN. So I—I—I may as well be saying good night.

CAROL. All right. Good night, Martin.

MARTIN (*crossing up* L *to the door*) Good night, Carol.

CAROL. And thanks for finding out about the pool.

MARTIN. Not at all. I'm very glad. Very glad, indeed—for *your* sake.

(MARTIN *goes out.* CAROL *stands until she hears the front door slam, then runs to the window.*

JACKY *enters up* L. *She is wearing her blazer*)

CAROL. If anyone wants me, Jacky, I'm in my room.

(JACKY *nods silently.* CAROL *goes out up* L *looking very miserable.* JACKY *stands motionless. It is obvious that something is wrong. Suddenly she bursts into tears and throws herself on to the sofa.*

MARTHA *enters with a tray to clear the tea things.* JACKY *tries to stop crying*)

MARTHA (*coming to the table*) Hello, Miss Jacky, all alone? Isn't it wonderful?

JACKY (*sniffing loudly*) Um!

MARTHA. Why, what's the matter, Miss Jacky? (*She crosses up* R *to collect the cup and plate from the small table by the armchair*)

JACKY. Nothing, I . . . (*Suddenly*) Oh, Martha, I'm in most terrible trouble.

MARTHA. Trouble? You?

JACKY (*rising*) I simply must tell someone—only will you promise not to tell a living soul?

MARTHA. Yes, Miss Jacky. If you don't want me to.

JACKY. It's awful. They all think they've won thousands of pounds.

MARTHA. Yes?

JACKY. Well, they haven't!

MARTHA. But they *have*, Miss Jacky!

JACKY. No, Martha. (*She pulls an envelope from her blazer pocket*) I've just found this.

MARTHA (*peering at it*) Well? What is it?

JACKY. It's the coupon. I didn't post it!

QUICK CURTAIN

ACT II

SCENE—*The same. The following morning.*
The curtains are open and it is fine and sunny outside.

When the CURTAIN *rises,* DENIS *is speaking on the telephone.*

DENIS. Oh, he's not? . . . You mean Mr Tranter hasn't been back all night? Very well, ask him to ring me when he gets in, would you? Mr Stafford . . . Denis Stafford . . . Thanks!

(*As he replaces the receiver,* PHILIP *enters*)

PHILIP. Hello, Denis.
DENIS. Hello, Dad! Lovely morning, isn't it?
PHILIP. I'll say it is. (*He crosses above the table to the window*) It would have to be pretty putrid not to be a lovely morning *this* morning, wouldn't it?
DENIS (*indicating Philip's clothes*) Going golfing? (*He crosses to* L *of the table*)
PHILIP. Yes. Care for a round?
DENIS. No, I don't think I'd be able to concentrate—not till we know how much we've clicked for. Besides, I've a phone call coming through.
PHILIP (*crossing down* R *to the fire*) I want to get to the club-house pretty early so as to withdraw my resignation.
DENIS. Your resignation? (*He crosses* R *below the table*)
PHILIP. Didn't you know? I wrote out my resignation yesterday afternoon.
DENIS. Whatever for?
PHILIP (*picking up a putter from below the fireplace*) Finance, old lad. I wasn't going to tell anybody here but, as a matter of fact, I had rather a chilly letter from Dobson yesterday morning.
DENIS. The Bank?
PHILIP. The old overdraft, you know! Said I was over my limit.
DENIS (*sitting on the back of the sofa*) I thought you looked a bit browned off.
PHILIP. Felt it, too! Don't know what I should have done without the golf club.
DENIS. Well, there's no need to worry about it *now*, is there?
PHILIP. No, thank God. (*He looks at his clothes*) Think I shall treat myself to a couple of new suits, too. (*He commences to practise imaginary putts*)
DENIS. You'll have to dig out a new tailor. Your man retired last year.

PHILIP. Oh yes, so he did.

DENIS. But I'll put you on to mine. So why worry?

PHILIP. Exactly. (*He flourishes the putter*) Why worry? D'you know, old son, it's an extraordinarily pleasant thing to be able to say "Why worry?" And *mean* it!

DENIS. We mustn't forget to send in the coupon copy. Registered letter, it's got to be, hasn't it?

PHILIP (*practising putting again*) Yes. I've sent the telegram.

DENIS. You've done what?

PHILIP. Sent the telegram. Didn't you know? You have to send a wire with your name and number and register your claim.

DENIS. But—damn it—I've done that! I phoned it through last night.

PHILIP (*amused*) And I've phoned through another one this morning!

DENIS. Well, I don't suppose it matters. (*He strolls up to the window*) Hello, what's Jacky doing out there?

PHILIP (*putting down his golf club and joining him at the window*) Jacky?

DENIS. Yes. Sitting on the garden seat on a bitter morning like this.

PHILIP. No coat on, either! She'll catch her death! (*He opens the window a bit*) Hey! Jacky!

(*There is a pause and then* JACKY *appears at the window. She looks cold and depressed*)

JACKY. Yes, Uncle Philip!

PHILIP. For goodness' sake come inside, Jacky.

(JACKY *enters and he closes the window*)

It's a bitter morning and you've no coat. What were you doing?

JACKY (*moving down to the fire*) Just thinking, Uncle Philip!

PHILIP (*following her*) Then I should choose a warmer spot than the garden seat. Aren't you frozen?

JACKY. I *am* rather cold, now you mention it. (*She sits on the stool down* R)

PHILIP. Now I mention it. You'll get pneumonia or something, and you don't want to be in bed for Christmas, do you?

JACKY. I really don't care—I mean, of course not!

PHILIP. Especially this Christmas. (*Looking at her*) Is anything the matter, Jacky?

JACKY. No. No, of course not.

PHILIP. You don't look your bright self, I must say. (*Crossing towards the phone*) Would you like me to ring up Macaulay?

JACKY (*quickly*) No, Uncle Philip—please don't! No doctor can do *me* any good—I mean—I'm quite all right, thank you.

PHILIP. Well, you don't look it. Think I'd better put your aunt on your track.

(PHILIP *exits up* L)

DENIS (*at the window*) Are you staying here for a bit?
JACKY (*in a panic*) Staying here?
DENIS. In the room, I mean.
JACKY. I suppose so.
DENIS. Then if the phone rings for me, give me a shout, will you?
JACKY. Yes.
DENIS (*crossing to the door up* L) I bet I know what's the matter with *you*.
JACKY (*turning quickly*) You do?
DENIS. Yes. You've fallen in love with the Manager of the Odeon.

(DENIS *exits up* L. *Left alone,* JACKY *tries to warm herself at the fire. She takes an envelope from her jacket pocket, looks at it despondently and puts it back again. She gives two loud sniffs and then turns round guiltily as the door up* L *opens and* MARTHA *enters with an armful of logs.* MARTHA *crosses to the fire, places the logs in the grate and then turns to regard* JACKY, *who has seated herself in an abject fashion on the sofa*)

MARTHA. Have you told them yet, Miss Jacky?
JACKY (*with a dismal shake of her head*) No.
MARTHA. You're quite sure, I suppose——?
JACKY. That I didn't post it? Of course I am. (*She produces the envelope*) Here it is! I really don't know how it could have happened. Aunt Ruth gave me a lot of letters to post and then Carol gave me the football letter, too. And I went straight across the road at the top of Church Hill and posted them.
MARTHA. One of them must have got left in your pocket.
JACKY. I know. By why had it got to be this one? (*She puts the envelope away*) Oh, Martha, what am I going to do?
MARTHA. You take my advice and tell them as soon as possible. Goodness knows what they might get up to—buying motorcars or something.
JACKY. They can't do anything desperate on a Sunday.
MARTHA. You never know. People can do desperate things on any day of the week.
JACKY. All right, Martha. I'll tell them.
MARTHA. Good. (*She crosses up* C)
JACKY. This afternoon.
MARTHA. Well, it's your affair, Miss Jacky . . .

(*The door opens and* CAROL *enters with a Sunday paper which she puts on the table*)

CAROL. Hello, Jacky. Are you better?
JACKY. I'm not ill, Carol.
CAROL. Well, you looked it when you left the breakfast table—positively green.

(MARTHA *exits up* L)

JACKY. It was nothing.
CAROL. Where are father and Denis?
JACKY. I think Uncle Philip has gone to find Aunt Ruth, and Denis is somewhere about. I'm guarding the telephone for him.
CAROL. I suppose I may as well go to church. There's nothing else to do. (*She moves towards the door up* L)
JACKY. Carol!
CAROL (*turning*) Yes?
JACKY. About Martin——
CAROL (*defensively*) *What* about Martin?
JACKY. Did he propose to you last night?
CAROL. Of course he didn't. (*She moves quickly* C) What makes you think he was *going* to propose to me?
JACKY. Because I told him to.
CAROL. You—told—him—to?
JACKY. Yes. I had an awful job to persuade him, but in the end he promised.
CAROL (*coming down* R *of the table*) Look here, Jacky, I don't know what you've been up to, but you'd better explain.
JACKY. Well, last night we were talking—Martin and I—and it was clear to me that he was as sick as mud and I guessed it was about you. And so I got it out of him.
CAROL. What did he say? (*She sits on the sofa, down stage of Jacky*)
JACKY. He admitted he was in love with you and that the only reason he didn't ask you to marry him was because he didn't think he could provide for you . . . And I pointed out to him that he was a chump, and in the end he saw it, too.
CAROL. And he said he was going to ask me to marry him?
JACKY. He promised—promised faithfully.
CAROL. Then what could have happened?
JACKY. I suppose he lost his nerve again. He hasn't got much guts, has he?
CAROL. Jacky!
JACKY. Sorry!
CAROL. It was very wrong of you to interfere, Jacky, but well, I suppose you meant well. If he really wants to marry me I suppose it will be all right—one day. (*Rising*) I feel better now. I don't think I'll go to church after all. (*She moves up* C)

(PHILIP *enters up* L, *followed by* DENIS)

DENIS (*moving down to the desk*) No phone calls?

JACKY. No, Denis.
CAROL. By the way, Father, I sent off the telegram.
PHILIP (*coming* C *behind the table*) What telegram?
CAROL. To Imperials, of course, to establish the claim. I phoned it through early this morning.
PHILIP. Heavens above! But I've sent one and so has Denis.
CAROL. Sorry. I didn't know. They won't disqualify us for it, will they?
DENIS. Of course not.

(RUTH *enters up* L *with a bowl of flowers*)

Here's Mother. (*Joking*) I bet she's sent one, too.
RUTH (*putting flowers on the table*) Sent one what, Denis dear?
PHILIP (*also joking*) A telegram to Imperials.
RUTH. Yes, dear, of course I have!
PHILIP }
DENIS } (*together*) *What!*

(DENIS *sits on the chair at the desk*)

RUTH. There's no need to worry. I sent it myself. I woke up in the middle of the night and remembered something Denis said about it last evening. So I got up and read the rules and phoned through a wire right away. About three o'clock this morning. I knew you'd forget about it. Nobody in this house ever remembers anything except me.
PHILIP. But my dear woman, we didn't forget. I've sent one. Denis has sent one, and so has Carol.
RUTH (*crossing in front of the table to the fire*) What a waste of money and the telephone account was very high last quarter as it was.
CAROL. Imperials will be furious!
RUTH. They can't possibly be angry with what I sent. I was most polite.
PHILIP. What did *you* send?
RUTH. I said "Please note we've won the cricket pool——"
DENIS (*jumping up*) Cricket!
RUTH. No, no. Football, of course! I'm sure I put "football". Cricket wouldn't make sense, would it?
DENIS. No, Mother dear. (*He sits again*)
RUTH. Then I expect I put "football". (*She crosses in front of the sofa to down* L *of the table*) I said "Please note we've won the football pool. I hope it's hundreds and thousands—I mean—hundreds *of* thousands. Kind regards."
DENIS. Why not "love and kisses"?
RUTH (*turning to him*) I didn't think that was necessary, dear.
PHILIP (*crossing below the sofa to the fire*) Imperials will think we're stark, staring mad.

DENIS. Let's hope some of those wires don't get through. They *may* not. You know what the telegraph service is like these days.

RUTH. Yes, Denis. (*With a sudden move towards the telephone*) Do you think we ought to send another?

DENIS (*rising, intercepting her and placing her in the desk chair*) No, Mother. I think it's a legitimate risk we must be prepared to accept.

RUTH. Just as you think, dear. Only it would be awful if there was a mistake, wouldn't it?

CAROL. I think I'd better go and warn Martha or else she'll be wiring, too.

(CAROL *exits up* L)

PHILIP (*to Jacky; dolefully*) I don't suppose you've sent a telegram, Jacky?

JACKY. No, Uncle Philip. (*She rises*) I haven't. I—I——

(JACKY *bursts into tears and rushes from the room by the door up* L)

PHILIP (*moving to* RC) What on earth's the matter with the girl this morning?

RUTH (*picking up some Christmas cards from the desk*) Jacky? Oh, I expect she's eaten something that's upset her.

PHILIP. She hardly touched her breakfast.

RUTH. There you are, you see! I'll make her have some calomel if she's not better.

DENIS (*going towards the door up* L) Let me know if there's a phone call.

PHILIP. I'm going to golf very soon.

DENIS. All right. I'll hear it upstairs, I expect.

(DENIS *exits up* L)

RUTH (*busy with the Christmas cards*) Did you say you were going to play golf, dear?

PHILIP (*moving below the table to* LC) Doubt if I'll play much. But I want to show up early at the clubhouse in order to withdraw the resignation I put in yesterday.

RUTH. Oh, yes, of course. I'm so glad you haven't to resign after all.

PHILIP. Me, too! As a matter of fact, I've been thinking and I've come to the conclusion that it might be a good idea to apply for life membership.

RUTH. Of the golf club?

PHILIP. Yes. There's a rule, you know. If you've been a member for ten years you can put down a lump sum—seventy-five pounds, I think it is—and then you're a member for life.

RUTH (*rising*) Wouldn't that be rather a waste of money?

PHILIP. No. On the contrary, I should say. (*Half joking*) Or do you think I'm marked down for an early grave?

RUTH (*moving a little towards him*) No, dear. I didn't mean that.

You're fifty-seven, I know, but there's no reason why you shouldn't live to be sixty-five or seventy—that is, if you take care.

PHILIP (*rather grim*) Thanks.

RUTH. Although, of course, I know the men in your family die young. What I mean, dear, is that it would be a waste of money to be a life member of the golf club when you won't be here to play.

PHILIP. What do you mean—not here to play?

RUTH. Well, dear, now you've won all the money, we shall be leaving, shan't we?

PHILIP. Leaving Caterham? Leaving this house?

RUTH (*crossing in front of him to the fire*) I've always wanted to live by the sea. I said so when we were on our honeymoon, even.

PHILIP. But, Ruth—— (*He follows her a pace*)

RUTH (*arranging some cards on the mantelpiece*) I've never made a secret of it. Of course, it was impossible when you were working in the city. I understand that. And it was impossible, too, when you retired because we couldn't afford it. But it's different now.

PHILIP. I don't see how?

RUTH. And you've always agreed with me that it would be nice to live at Bournemouth. Time after time you've agreed and said that perhaps one day the ship would come home. Now it has come home.

PHILIP (*crossing to* C *below the table*) But I *hate* Bournemouth!

RUTH (*still arranging the cards*) Seaton, or Torquay, then. I don't really mind which.

PHILIP. I hate Seaton and I hate Torquay, too! (*He moves to the back of the sofa*) Now, look here, Ruth! I don't want to leave this house and I don't want to leave Caterham, either.

RUTH. Why not, dear?

PHILIP. Well, there's the golf club, for one thing.

RUTH (*turning to face him*) But there are some nice golf clubs at Bournemouth, Philip. You played there once. Don't you remember? You hit a ball through a window of one of those pretty houses.

PHILIP (*crossing to* LC) But I don't want to play golf at Bournemouth. (*Turning*) You don't understand! Golf isn't just a matter of merely hitting a white ball into a small hole.

RUTH. Isn't it, Philip? I always thought that was the *idea* of the game.

PHILIP. What I mean is that it's the friendships you make.

RUTH. I don't see why you couldn't be just as friendly at Bournemouth or Seaton as at Caterham. And yesterday you were thinking of resigning from the club—did resign, in fact—so it couldn't mean so much to you as all that!

PHILIP. Not mean so much to me! Don't you realize that last night I was nearly a broken man?

RUTH. Nonsense, dear! Don't be theatrical! (*She sits on the sofa*)

PHILIP. It's not nonsense!

RUTH. Why, when I said how sorry I was you were giving up the game you distinctly said it didn't matter.

PHILIP (*breaking to* C) Now isn't that just like a woman to say a thing like that?

RUTH. Why not? I *am* a woman!

PHILIP (*returning solemnly a pace and pausing*) Yesterday evening, for the sake of the family, I was prepared to make a great sacrifice. I was prepared to renounce something which probably meant more to me than anything else in life. And, because I hid my sufferings and because I didn't come home and moan and groan and insist on everyone sharing my misery, you jump to the conclusion that I didn't *care*.

RUTH. Of course, if you think more of your putting and masheeing than your own wife's happiness, then . . .

PHILIP (*crossing to* LC *and almost shouting*) Go on! I *knew* we should get to that, soon.

RUTH. Then if you *knew*, Philip, there's no need to pretend to be surprised. And you said just now it meant more than anything . . .

PHILIP (*striding up* L *of the table towards the window*) God give me patience!

RUTH. I wish he would! Although what you have to be patient about I really don't know. I'm one of those "green widows" you hear about!

PHILIP (*coming down* R *of the sofa to the fire and changing his tactics*) Now, look here, my dear . . .

RUTH. There's no need for me to look *anywhere*. It's perfectly obvious that you are quite content to go on playing golf and gossiping in the clubhouse with your drunken friends . . .

PHILIP (*angry again*) Drunken friends!

RUTH. You know perfectly well that Major Blackley was had up the other day for driving his car under the influence of drink. It was in the local paper.

PHILIP. What the devil has that to do with it?

RUTH. If he's capable of driving a car when he's drunk he's quite capable of driving a *ball*, too!

PHILIP. I doubt it!

RUTH. Please don't quibble. (*She starts to sob*) You don't care if your poor wife—the wife who has stood by you all these terrible years—has to go on living in a hovel.

PHILIP. A hovel? Are you suggesting that this house is a hovel? It's a delightful house. Don't you realize that today I could sell it for nearly twice as much as I gave for it?

RUTH. Then that's another very good reason for selling it and going to Bournemouth. And, as for it being a delightful house— well, it's no such thing! Whoever designed it should never have put the pantry facing south and the dining-room on the opposite side of the hall to the kitchen.

PHILIP (*crossing below the sofa to* R *of the table*) Little details like that . . .

RUTH. I quite realize they are details to *you*! You don't have to cook the food or serve the meals or try to prevent the milk from turning sour. A house to you is merely something you walk into—with muddy boots, often—and eat and sleep in until it's time to go back to your precious golf club. Of course, I always knew you were selfish, but . . .

PHILIP. Selfish! Me—selfish? (*He sits* R *of the table*)

RUTH. Yes, dear. I'm afraid you are. Look at the way you always monopolize the paper at breakfast!

PHILIP. I had no idea you *wanted* the paper at breakfast!

RUTH. No, dear, of course not! It never occurred to you that a woman may be a slave and a drudge and still be able to *read*!

PHILIP. Slave and drudge? You?

RUTH (*rising*) Yes, dear. Me! What else do you think I've been since I married you. Bringing up your children, pinching and scraping; worrying about pennies here and halfpennies there and standing in queues and having fly-bombs roaring over the house and . . .

PHILIP. I suppose you'll say I started the war, next!

RUTH. Well, you did very little to help *stop* it!

PHILIP. I was in the Home Guard!

RUTH. Yes, dear. With headquarters at the Golf Club! And you were very selfish, too, about the vicar's garden party. You knew I wanted to go and wear a new hat—not, of course, that I *had* one!

PHILIP. If you hadn't *got* one how could you *wear* it?

RUTH. Don't be illogical, Philip. (*She comes around the sofa to him*) And then there's your mother . . .

PHILIP. I admit she's been a trial but she's a trial to *both* of us.

RUTH. You can go out and leave her but I can't. Now, when you win a fortune all you think about is going out and buying the golf club.

PHILIP. I never said anything at all about *buying* the golf club!

RUTH. Becoming a member, then—it's the same thing. (*She turns away and begins to cry*)

PHILIP (*rising slowly—very shaken*) This is a revelation to me, Ruth. We've been married nearly thirty years now, and until today we've never had a serious quarrel—hardly a cross word, even. I had no idea that, all the time, you had been harbouring all those brutal things against me.

RUTH. Because, for once, I cease to flatter you, I'm being brutal, I suppose.

PHILIP (*turning away* L) I didn't say *you* were being brutal. I said you were accusing me of being brutal.

RUTH. So you are. Very brutal and very *selfish*, too!

PHILIP (*walking up and down, waving his arms*) Just because I don't want to pull myself up by the roots and rush off to some horrid seaside resort full of trippers with ice cream cones, waving lobsters, some rotten place decked out with marine parades and oriental piers and public lavatories . . .

RUTH. Don't be indecent!

PHILIP (*now up* L *of the table*) Just because I want to enjoy a bit of peace and quiet for once, free from worry and take things easy in a reasonable and enjoyable way, you say I am brutal and selfish. I didn't know you *hated* me so.

RUTH (*tearfully*) I don't hate you. (*She sits* R *of the table*) A woman can see a man's faults without hating him. All this awful scene just because I want to live in a nice house at Bournemouth and have a chalet on the beach where we can have tea.

PHILIP (*crossing behind the table to* RC) And listen to the concert party crooners! (*Turning to her*) It's time you grew up, Ruth. Goodness knows, you're old enough!

RUTH. So I'm a hag now, am I? You're a brute, Philip—that's what you are—a brute! And I *hate* you!

PHILIP (*trying to pacify her*) Now, look here, old thing . . .

RUTH. Go away! Go away to your golf club and *get drunk*!

(GRANDMA *enters*)

GRANDMA. Oh, so *here* you are, Philip! Are you going to church?

PHILIP (*loudly*) No! I'm not! (*He stamps away to the fire*)

GRANDMA (*crossing to the armchair above the fireplace*) No need to shout. I merely thought that, in the circumstances, you might be going to count your blessings.

PHILIP (*dangerously quiet*) Count my what?

GRANDMA. Blessings!

PHILIP (*with an angry glance at Ruth*) Well—I'm not.

GRANDMA. I don't suppose Denis will be going, either.

PHILIP. I should think it's most unlikely.

GRANDMA. That means the car won't be going.

PHILIP. No, Grandma. But it's a nice morning if you want to walk.

GRANDMA. Oh, it's all right, Philip. I've lived here long enough to know that nobody bothers about me! I only hope that when we move to Bournemouth we shall be nearer a place of worship.

PHILIP (*after a pause*) When we do *what*?

GRANDMA. When we move to Bournemouth—that's what I said.

PHILIP. And who says we're moving to Bournemouth?

GRANDMA. Ruth. We were talking about it after breakfast. And a very good idea, too. I *like* Bournemouth, and I've some friends there—three sisters by the name of Winkworth. It will be nice to have them to tea on Sundays.

PHILIP. I dare say it would, but we're not *going* to live at Bournemouth!

GRANDMA. Why not?
PHILIP (*charging up to the window*) Because I hate Bournemouth and I wouldn't be found dead in Bournemouth.
RUTH. We're not asking you to be found dead there, Philip. We're asking you to live there.
PHILIP. It's the same thing so far as I'm concerned.
GRANDMA. What's the matter?
RUTH. Well may you ask, Grandma. Just because I suggested we should all like to live at Bournemouth, Philip has flown into one of his awful tempers. Just now he called me a lobster!
PHILIP (*swinging back to above the table*) I didn't call you a lobster!
RUTH. Yes, you did! You said I was a lobster—waving an ice cream cone!
PHILIP (*in a rage again*) I said nothing of the sort. I . . .
RUTH. Did you mention lobsters, or did you *not*, Philip?
PHILIP (*coming round to* L *of the table*) I only said that lobsters . . .
RUTH (*to Grandma*) There you are, you see!
PHILIP. I said that Bournemouth was full of lobsters waving— I mean *trippers* with lobsters waving—that is—oh, *hell!* (*He sits* L *of the table*)
RUTH. I've already asked you not to swear.
GRANDMA. I should think not, indeed. And on a Sunday morning, too!
PHILIP (*holding his head in his hands*) I don't care if it's Sunday morning or Friday afternoon! I feel like swearing and I shall swear just as much as I like!
RUTH. Of course you will, Philip. I realize only too well that you've no sense of shame.
PHILIP (*gasping*) Shame!
RUTH (*to Grandma*) I really don't know what's come over Philip. (*She rises, moves to the sofa, and sits on the upstage end*) Winning all this money has made him more selfish than ever.
GRANDMA. He always *was* selfish. Even as a small child he was selfish. Paul and Maud had much nicer characters. (*To Ruth*) He's got much worse since he married and I must say it's largely your fault, Ruth. You've always given in to his whims and fancies.
RUTH (*to Grandma*) Yes, dear, I'm afraid I have.
PHILIP. "Yes, dear!" I never thought I'd live to see you two ganging up against me!
RUTH. Ganging up! What an expression!
GRANDMA. I expect he learned it from that Jacky at the bioscope.
PHILIP (*jumping up and crossing to the back of the sofa*) Now, about this Bournemouth nonsense. Let's get it settled for once and for all.
RUTH. It *is* settled. The money's in your name and not in mine.

All I asked was that I could pass my few remaining years at a nice seaside resort—(*she sobs*) and have a little enjoyment.

(PHILIP *turns away in despair and sits* R *of the table*)

But, of course, I can't force you to and so you will go on being brutal and selfish and swearing at lobsters and ... (*She dissolves into tears*)

GRANDMA (*going to her*) There, there, there! Come with me, my dear, and we'll make a nice strong cup of tea.

(GRANDMA *leads* RUTH *to the door up* L *and opens it.* RUTH *goes out.* GRANDMA *turns in the doorway*)

Crippen!

(GRANDMA *goes out*)

PHILIP. Crippen! (*He jumps up, crosses to the door and shouts after her*) What the hell's Crippen got to do with it? (*He is about to exit but changes his mind and stamps back to* RC) Bournemouth, indeed! Seaton! Torquay! Damn!

(*The telephone rings*)

And damn you, too! (*He goes to the phone and lifts the receiver*) Hello. Yes, it is! ... Who? What? ... Hold on, will you?

(PHILIP *is about to put down the phone when* DENIS *hurries in*)

DENIS. Was that the phone?
PHILIP. Yes, for you. (*He hands* DENIS *the receiver*)
DENIS. Good! Hello! Is that you, Eric? I've been trying ...
PHILIP. Denis! Do you want to live at Bournemouth?
DENIS. Do I *what?* Shut up, Dad, can't you see I'm on the phone? (*He speaks into the receiver*) Hello, Eric ...
PHILIP (*gripping Denis's arm*) Do-you-want-to-live-at-Bournemouth?
DENIS. What? For heaven's sake—of course I don't want to live at Bournemouth.
PHILIP. That's all right, then! (*He crosses towards the fire, filling his pipe*)
DENIS (*glaring at him*) What's all right? (*He speaks into the receiver*) Hello, old man. Sorry, I ... Bournemouth? No, I was speaking to the guv'nor. Afraid the old boy's gone a bit dippy ...

(PHILIP *turns in amazement*)

Now, listen Eric, it's all right ... I'm in! I'm definitely in on this ... Yes, the full five hundred ... a fifty-fifty partnership ... Eh? ... No, I doubt if I can manage that ... Not till the end of the week at the earliest ... Damn! That's awkward. I tell you what I *can* do. I can let you have one-fifty right away and the balance later ... Yes, I've one-fifty of that money left me. I can send you a cheque right away. How will that do? . . . Splendid! Grand, old boy. Yes . . . Yes . . . You'll have it first thing in the morning. Right. Bye-bye, old boy . . . Yes . . Cheerio! (*He replaces the receiver and comes down* C *rubbing his hands with satisfaction*) So that's that! Thank God I managed to contact old Eric in time. It would have broken my heart if I'd missed this chance.

PHILIP (*who has lit his pipe and sat on the stool down* R) Something good?

DENIS (*very pleased*) You bet! This won't half be a surprise to Perkins and Perkins.

PHILIP. What will.

DENIS. My resignation, of course!

PHILIP. You're chucking your job in the City?

DENIS (*sitting on the back of the sofa*) Not half!

PHILIP. But do you think that's wise, old son?

DENIS. Well, my share's bound to be more than three-fifty. And that's all I need to go in with Eric.

PHILIP. But what sort of business is it? I mean, is it a business you know anything about?

DENIS. It's quite simple. I soon will.

PHILIP. Yes, old son, but what sort of business?

DENIS (*rising to* RC) Well—er—it's a bit complicated, really, and . . .

PHILIP. You just said it was quite simple.

DENIS. I mean, complicated to explain.

PHILIP. All the same, I wish you'd tell me. I've had a lot of experience in the City, you know.

DENIS. This is not in the City. (*He hesitates*) Well, there's no secret about it. (*He crosses and sits on the sofa*) Fact is, old Eric has got on to a damn good thing. He has a cousin who lives down in Berkshire—quite close to an ordnance dump left over from the last war. You know what the government is like—forget all about these places and allow everything to go to rust and ruin. Some of the stuff is still pretty good though—tyres, spare parts and motoring gadgets. Eric and his cousin have an option to take the place over but not enough ready money handy so Eric's offered to let me in fifty-fifty with him.

PHILIP. Yes, but—sounds a bit queer to me.

DENIS. What's queer about it?

PHILIP. Why doesn't Eric's cousin deal directly with the big motor firms himself? Why is he letting *you* in on it?

DENIS. Oh, I don't know. Why shouldn't he? According to Eric this cousin is a bit of a dope. Probably doesn't see the potentialities of the thing. Rather like poor old Martin, next door —content to make small money and leave the big stuff to people prepared to take a chance.

PHILIP. So there's a chance in it, is there?

DENIS. There's a chance in everything, I suppose.

PHILIP. And how much is your friend, Eric Tranter, chancing? If his scheme is as good as you say it is he wouldn't be touting it about all over the place.

DENIS (*rising in a temper*) Touting it about, my foot! Eric wants to do me a good turn. We did our service in the R.A.F. together.

PHILIP. I had a pal in the same platoon in World War One and he ran off with the girl I was engaged to. (*Suddenly*) I say, you needn't tell your mother that!

DENIS. The last war was different. (*He moves up* RC)

PHILIP. *All* wars are different—till they're over. (*He rises*) Now you be sensible, old son. Ring Tranter and tell him it's all off.

DENIS. No. My mind's made up. This is a chance of a lifetime and I'm not going to let it slip. My cheque goes off today.

PHILIP. Be guided by me, Denis . . .

DENIS (*behind the table*) Why should I? Did you always do what your father advised?

PHILIP (*moving down* RC) No.

DENIS. There you are, you see.

PHILIP. But afterwards I often wished I had done. I'm older than you, old lad.

DENIS. For God's sake—what's that got to do with it? (*He moves down* L *of the table*) You want to see me lead a stick-in-the-mud humdrum existence like that poor sucker, Martin Latham.

PHILIP. I don't think Martin Latham is a sucker. I think he's pretty shrewd and has his head screwed on the right way.

DENIS. I'm not going to spend my life in one of those "Yes, sir —no, sir, three bags full" sort of jobs. You don't understand, Dad!

PHILIP. Oh, yes, I do. (*He crosses to* C *below the table*) You're restless, and it's only natural, you've been living an out-of-door, free-for-all kind of life and you're finding it hard to settle down again.

DENIS. The only real thing you've got against my scheme is that you don't like Eric Tranter.

PHILIP (*moving a little towards the fire*) No, it's more than that. (*He turns*) I've a feeling that there may be something—well, dishonest, about it.

DENIS. So what?

PHILIP (*shocked*) My dear Denis!

DENIS. Suppose it is a bit of a wangle? What's it matter if we don't get spotted? *All* trading and barter bargaining is dishonest at rock bottom, it's a battle of wits.

PHILIP. All the same . . .

DENIS. What's the use of talking? We don't speak the same language! I'm going ahead with this. (*He strides up* L *to the window*)

PHILIP (*following him*) Now listen to me, Denis . . .

DENIS (*dangerously*) Well?

PHILIP (R *of him at the window*) I forbid you to go into this scheme. I'm still your father, you know.

DENIS. Yes, and I'm not a kid at school to be told what to do and what not to do. Winning the pool has given me a chance and I'm going to take it.

PHILIP. So long as you're under my roof . . .

DENIS (*angrily*) Oh, so that's it, is it? Very well, then. I'll clear out!

PHILIP. Denis—I . . .

DENIS. Eric has a spare room—I'll move in tomorrow!

PHILIP (*trying to take his arm*) Now, look here, my boy . . .

DENIS (*shaking him off*) I've had it so far as home life is concerned! Now I'm going to write out that cheque.

PHILIP. Denis, for the last time . . .

DENIS. No, Dad—the last time's done with.

(DENIS *reaches the door up* L. *As he does so*, RUTH *enters*)

RUTH. Oh, here you are, Denis. I don't suppose you'd care to get the car out and drive Grandma to church?

DENIS. Sorry, Mother. I'm busy.

(DENIS *goes out*)

RUTH. It isn't much to ask, dear, and . . . (*She is about to follow* Denis)

PHILIP. I say, Ruth!

RUTH (*very coldly*) Yes?

PHILIP (*moving down* RC) Don't go for a minute. Close the door, I want to speak to you.

RUTH (*after closing the door*) Well:

PHILIP. I'm worried, Ruth—very worried, indeed.

RUTH (LC) I don't see why. You've had your own way about Bournemouth . . .

PHILIP. It's nothing to do with Bournemouth. For heaven's sake let's forget about Bournemouth and—it's to do with Denis.

RUTH (*still coldly*) Oh?

PHILIP. I'm desperately worried about him. He's getting himself mixed up in some wild-cat scheme with Eric Tranter. I don't like it and before it's all over Denis will lose five hundred pounds.

RUTH. Denis hasn't got five hundred pounds.

PHILIP. No, but he will have. He's sending off a cheque for one-fifty now. He's getting mixed up with a gang of crooks who'll have his shirt off him before he's finished.

RUTH. Then why don't you stop him?

PHILIP. I've tried. It's no good. I went so far as to forbid him to have anything to do with it, and *then* what do you think happened?

RUTH (*indifferently*) I've no idea.

PHILIP. He said he should leave home.

RUTH. Leave home?

PHILIP. Yes. He's going to live in the same house as this Tranter fellow.

RUTH. You're not serious?

PHILIP. I am. And so is *he*.

RUTH. This is a nice thing, I must say. Not content with being brutal and selfish to me—you now want to drive my son out of the house!

PHILIP. I want no such thing!

RUTH. Oh, yes, you do. I expect you called him a lobster or something.

PHILIP. I didn't. Anyway, I wish you'd talk to him.

RUTH. I will. (*She moves towards the door up* L) I shall tell him not to put up with your selfish and domineering ways.

(RUTH *goes out*)

PHILIP. Selfish and dom—— I'll be damned! (*He comes to the fire and stands in silence for a moment, then he moves across to the telephone*) I've a darned good mind to—no, I suppose it would only make it worse. (*He sits at the desk*)

(*The door opens and* JACKY *comes in. She does not see Philip. She crosses to the sofa, sits down and stares into the fire*)

Hello, Jacky.

JACKY (*starting guiltily*) Hello, Uncle Philip!

PHILIP. Feeling better?

JACKY. I'm all right, thank you, Uncle Philip.

PHILIP (*rising and crossing slowly towards her*) I suppose it's a good thing you've no share in this pool money or you'd be wanting to do something ridiculous, as well.

(JACKY *does not answer*)

Do you like Bournemouth?

JACKY (*shaking her head*) No.

PHILIP (*behind sofa*) Or Seaton or Torquay?

JACKY. No. I don't think I like any place very much.

PHILIP. Look here, Jacky. What is the matter with you?

JACKY. Nothing. Nothing at all, Uncle Philip.

PHILIP. Oh, yes, there is. You can't deceive me.

JACKY. Oh, Uncle Philip, I wish I could tell you.

PHILIP. Then why not?

JACKY. I can't.

PHILIP. Are you expecting a bad report from school?

JACKY. Not more than usual.

PHILIP. Then what is it?

JACKY. I—no, I can't tell you—yet.

PHILIP. Come along, now. We've never had any secrets.

JACKY. That's all you think!

PHILIP. Whatever it is I'll stand by you. Out with it!
JACKY (*in desperation*) Well—I—oh, Uncle Philip, I . . . (*She kneels up on the sofa*)

(CAROL *enters*)

CAROL. Oh, Jacky, do something for me, will you?
JACKY (*jumping up, all too eager to escape*) Of course, Carol. What is it? (*She crosses above the table to* C)

(PHILIP *goes to the fire*)

CAROL. Martin's walking up and down the garden next door. I've been watching him from my window; run out and ask him to come in, will you? Tell him Father wants to speak to him about something important.
PHILIP (*turning*) But I don't.
CAROL. No. But I *do*! Run on, Jacky.

(JACKY *goes out up* L)

PHILIP. I really don't know what's going on here this morning, but . . .
CAROL (*going to the window*) Oh, Daddy, darling, I'm so miserable!
PHILIP (*crossing above the sofa to* C) What? You, *too*! Just when we've had all this wonderful stroke of luck? I can't understand what's the matter with everybody. I've quarrelled with your mother for the first time in thirty years and now she won't speak to me. Your grandmother's called me a murderer. Denis wants to leave home, and you—what *is* your trouble, by the way?
CAROL (*breaking away to the window and looking out*) Hurry, darling, hurry! He's coming. (*She propels* PHILIP *towards the door down* L)
PHILIP. But I thought you wanted me to speak to him about something important?
CAROL. Not you—me! Hurry! (*She continues to push him out*)
PHILIP (*as he goes down* L) I'm giving up trying to sort things out. Lobsters, indeed!

(PHILIP *goes out down* L. CAROL *runs up and opens the window*)

CAROL (*calling*) Martin! You can come in this way!
MARTIN (*appearing at the window*) Hello!
CAROL. Come in!

(MARTIN *enters*. CAROL *closes the window*)

Good morning, Martin.
MARTIN (*uneasily*) Good morning, Carol.
CAROL (*crossing down* R *of the sofa*) Come and sit down.
MARTIN (*standing up* RC) I mustn't stop. Jacky said Mr Stafford wanted to see me about something.

CAROL. Yes. Yes, that's right—something urgent.

MARTIN (*looking round the room*) Then . . .

CAROL. He'll be here in a minute. He was called to the telephone.

MARTIN (*swinging round to look at the telephone*) Eh?

CAROL (*covering her blunder*) I mean, he *will* be called to the telephone—about some business matter. (*She crosses to him*) I expect that's what he wants to see you about. He's gone to his study to get the—the papers.

MARTIN (*making a move towards the door down* L) Then, in that case I'd better . . .

CAROL (*interrupting him*) No, no! He particularly wanted you to wait for him in here. Do sit down!

MARTIN. Very well. (*He sits very unhappily* R *of the table*) I hope he won't be long. I—I'm in the middle of writing an important letter.

CAROL (L *of the table*) But you've been walking up and down the garden for the past half-hour. I've been watching you.

MARTIN. I—I couldn't think of anything to say.

CAROL. In the letter?

MARTIN. Yes, in the letter, of course.

(CAROL *sits in the chair above the table*)

CAROL (*after a pause*) Martin!

MARTIN. Yes?

CAROL. What's the matter? Are you angry with me?

MARTIN. Good heavens, no!

CAROL. I thought when you didn't come to hockey yesterday afternoon I must have offended you.

MARTIN. No. No. Not at all.

CAROL. Then, when you came in last night, I realized I hadn't. You seemed like your old self again.

MARTIN. Oh!

CAROL. Your own *sweet* self.

MARTIN. I—I—— (*Evadingly*) Do you think Mr Stafford will be long? (*He half rises*)

CAROL. Never mind about him now, Martin.

MARTIN (*slowly sitting again*) But you said it was urgent and . . .

CAROL. What I want to say is urgent, too. What's gone wrong between you and me? We used to be such good friends.

MARTIN. We still *are*, aren't we? (*He pauses*) At least, I hope so.

CAROL. So do I, Martin. (*She pauses*) I wondered if you'd got engaged to someone.

MARTIN. What!

CAROL. To some girl who wouldn't like us going on being friends. I wondered if this was what you were going to tell me last night. Don't you remember? You said you wanted to ask me something and then, before you did, Mother came in.

MARTIN. Yes. Yes. So she did!
CAROL. And you *didn't* ask me.
MARTIN. No. No. I didn't.
CAROL. Then you *weren't* going to tell me you'd got engaged?
MARTIN. No. You see, I *hadn't*.
CAROL. I'm glad, Martin.
MARTIN. So am I!
CAROL (*after a pause she rises and moves round to* L *of him*) Do you know what Jacky thought?
MARTIN. Jacky?
CAROL. She thought you were going to propose to me.
MARTIN. Good Lord! I wouldn't dream of doing such a thing!
CAROL (*turning away*) I see.
MARTIN. Here, I say! I don't mean that—that——(*He stops*)
CAROL. I'm not offended, Martin. What you mean is that you've never felt about me in that way?
MARTIN (*rising*) I—I think I'd better go now and—er—call back later.
CAROL (*pushing him back into his chair*) No. Don't go. Father will be awfully cross if he finds you've gone.
MARTIN. But—very well.
CAROL. Then you never *have* felt about me in—that way?
MARTIN. I—I—— (*In a strangled voice*) You're making it very difficult for me, Carol.
CAROL. I'm sorry. I'm not trying to, of course. I can see now that Jacky was quite wrong. (*She turns and sits at the desk*)
MARTIN. She wasn't.
CAROL. Do you mean you *still* want to marry me?
MARTIN. It's impossible. I'm going abroad!
CAROL. *You*—going abroad?
MARTIN. Yes, I couldn't bear going on living at Caterham—in England, even—so, I'm going abroad.
CAROL. What on earth for?
MARTIN. To try and forget you, of course. It—it won't be easy.
CAROL. Then why try? Why do you want to forget me? You talk as if you'd asked me to marry you and I'd refused.
MARTIN. Do I?
CAROL. And I haven't.
MARTIN. Of course not. I didn't ask you.
CAROL. Why *didn't* you?
MARTIN. Because it's impossible. Don't you see? You winning all that money. I can't possibly ask you to marry me now you're a rich woman.
CAROL. Why not?
MARTIN. It wouldn't be honourable. People would say I was only marrying you for your money.

CAROL. Thank you.

MARTIN. I mean—people would say—not that it would be true, of course—but—all the same . . .

CAROL (*rising*) Martin Latham! I think you're a fool! (*She goes up stage*)

MARTIN. Me?

CAROL (*turning*) Yes. You!

MARTIN (*offended*) I don't think it very fair of you to call me a fool just because I'm trying to do the right thing.

CAROL. Right thing my . . . (*She breaks off and comes down* L *of him*) Listen to me, you poor boob . . .

MARTIN. What!

CAROL. Don't you realize that, if people love each other, nothing else matters?

MARTIN. That's what Jacky said, but . . .

CAROL (*getting angry*) Jacky! (*Crossing behind the table to up* R) I suppose you would never even have thought of asking me to marry you if Jacky hadn't made you promise her?

MARTIN. Yes. That's right.

CAROL (*returning to* L *of the table*) Now listen to me, Martin Latham! If you had asked me to marry you I should have said "No"!

MARTIN. But just now you said . . .

CAROL (*sweeping on*) Do you think that a girl has no pride? Do you think a girl would agree to marry a spineless chump like you just because he'd been egged on to propose to her by a picture-minded school kid?

MARTIN (*gloomily*) So I'm a spineless chump, am I?

CAROL. Yes. You are!

MARTIN. And if I'd asked you to marry me last night, you'd have refused me?

CAROL. Yes, I should.

MARTIN. Oh! Oh, I see. (*Very gloomily*) Then everything's all right?

CAROL (*exasperated beyond control*) It's—it's *magnificent*!

MARTIN (*rising*) Then this is—good-bye?

CAROL. Definitely! (*She crosses up to the window*)

MARTIN (*following up to* L *of her*) Well—good-bye, then, Carol. I shall go abroad.

CAROL. You can go to the devil so far as I'm concerned!

(*The door down* L *opens and* PHILIP *appears*)

PHILIP (*peeping into the room*) Is everything all right?

CAROL. All right!

PHILIP (*indicating his study*) There's no fire in there. And it's a cold morning. Is it all settled?

CAROL. Nothing has been *more* settled.

PHILIP (*moving across in front of the table to the fire*) Good! I'm glad *someone* is happy. Good morning, Martin. (*He warms his hands at the fire*)

MARTIN. Good morning, Mr Stafford. Will you tell me what it is you want to see me about as soon as you can? I think it's time I went.

PHILIP (*turning*) But I don't want to see you about anything. (*He indicates Carol*) It was ...

CAROL (*moving quickly to the upstage end of the sofa*) Of course you do, Father! You sent Jacky to *fetch* Martin.

PHILIP. Oh, yes, so I did. Let me see—what was it now?

MARTIN. Carol said it was urgent.

PHILIP. Oh, yes, very urgent indeed. Only I can't remember what it was. Silly of me.

(RUTH *enters up* L *with* GRANDMA. RUTH *has more Christmas cards*)

Ah, Ruth, dear, do you know what it was I wanted to see Martin about?

RUTH (*going down to the desk with the cards*) I haven't the slightest idea.

GRANDMA (*crossing and sitting in the armchair*) Something to do with buying the golf club—or something equally selfish.

(DENIS *enters up* L. *He has an envelope in his hand*)

DENIS. Hello, Martin.

MARTIN. Good morning.

DENIS (*above the table*) You're going to be darned sorry, old man, that you didn't take that chance I offered you. I've just fixed a fifty-fifty partnership with Eric Tranter and we're going to clean up a packet.

MARTIN. It wouldn't have been any good, anyway. I'm going abroad.

RUTH (*turning*) Going abroad, Martin. (*Moving to* L *of the table*) When?

MARTIN. As soon as I can arrange it.

RUTH. But—— (*To Carol*) Did you hear what he said?

CAROL. Yes. And the sooner he goes the better! (*She throws herself full length on the sofa and bursts into tears*)

RUTH (*hurrying to the back of the sofa*) My dear Carol! What is it?

CAROL (*screaming*) I hate him! I hate him! (*She continues to scream*)

DENIS (*seizing Martin by the arm and swinging him around*) What the devil have you been doing to my sister?

MARTIN. Nothing. Nothing. I assure you.

DENIS (*releasing him*) I don't know what's the matter with everyone this morning. (*He strides away down* R) I seem to be the only one who's kept his head about the football pool.

PHILIP (*crossing below the table to him*) On the contrary. It seems to me that you've been the first one to lose it. Once and for all, Denis, I beg you not to go into this foolish scheme.

DENIS. I'm in, Dad, so you may as well save your breath. I'm going out to post my cheque now. Here it is. (*He shows the envelope*)

PHILIP. For the last time, Denis—don't do it. (*He turns*) Ruth!

RUTH. Don't ask me to interfere! And when he's made a fortune I shall go and live at Bournemouth, whether you come or not.

PHILIP. Heavens above! We're back at Bournemouth! (*He crosses up to the window*)

(JACKY *enters up* L, *unobserved. She stands listening*)

RUTH. We're *not* at Bournemouth. We're still in Caterham. (*To Martin*) I hope, Martin, that when you come back from—from—wherever it is you're going, and marry Carol . . .

CAROL. Mother! Mother! (*She cries louder than ever and beats her fists on the sofa*)

RUTH. Or someone. I hope you'll take a lesson from what's happened here. I had no idea Philip could behave like this. I almost wish he'd never won the football pool.

PHILIP (*furiously*) Now you're talking sense. (*He comes level with Martin at* RC) I think you're quite right to go abroad, Martin, and not risk the chance of getting mixed up in a family like mine. We get a wonderful stroke of luck and look what happens! My own wife threatens to leave me. Denis proposes to get mixed up with a gang of scoundrels. My mother calls me names. Jacky is sick and Carol goes into hysterics! You're dead right, Ruth. I wish to God we'd never won that bloody pool! (*He thumps the table and sits behind it*)

JACKY (*coming forward to* LC) You haven't!

PHILIP (*turning suddenly*) What did you say?

(CAROL *stops screaming*)

JACKY. I said—you haven't!

DENIS. What do you mean?

JACKY (L *of Philip*) You haven't won the football pool. I forgot to post it.

DENIS ⎫
PHILIP ⎬ (*together*) What!
RUTH ⎪
CAROL ⎭

JACKY. I forgot to post it. (*She produces the envelope*) Here it is!

PHILIP. My God! (*He drops his head into his hands*)

(*There is silence for a moment. They are all too dumbfounded to speak*)

DENIS. Well. That's that! (*He tears his letter into pieces and throws it on the floor*)

(*Again there is silence.* GRANDMA *rises*)

GRANDMA. This is a judgement. (*She moves up* L *towards the door*)
RUTH. Grandma! Where are you going?
GRANDMA. Going? I'm going to pack, of course!

GRANDMA *goes out. They glare at one another as—*

the CURTAIN *falls*

ACT III

SCENE—*The same. About five o'clock on the following evening (Monday)*

When the CURTAIN *rises, the room is in half-light from window and fire.*
JACKY *can be seen sitting by the fire on the lower end of the sofa, when* MARTHA *enters up* L *and switches on the light.*

JACKY (*starting*) Who's that? Oh, it's you, Martha!
MARTHA. Yes, Miss Jacky. (*She crosses to the window and draws the curtains*) Feeling better, Miss Jacky?
JACKY. I don't know. People are funny, Martha. Yesterday morning, when it all happened, I thought it was just the right moment. Aunt Ruth said she wished they'd never won the pool, and Uncle Philip said he wished it, and Carol said she wished it, too! I thought they'd be glad when I told them. But they weren't!
MARTHA. Well, you could hardly expect it, could you?
JACKY. I didn't expect Denis to be glad because he had some scheme on and wanted the money. But the others . . .
MARTHA (*who has come down to the fire*) Nobody's been angry with you, have they? Not even Mr Denis.
JACKY. No.
MARTHA (*putting a log on the fire*) There you are, you see!
JACKY. Except Grandma.
MARTHA. Well, she's not here so I should forget about her. (*She takes a newspaper from the armchair and folds it*)
JACKY. Venomous old witch! That's the one really good thing —she's gone! It was terrible here yesterday afternoon and evening—the atmosphere. Denis went straight out and didn't come back till midnight. Carol sat in her room, crying. Grandma was upstairs, packing, and Uncle Philip and Aunt Ruth wouldn't speak to one another. It was awful.
MARTHA (*putting the paper on the stool*) They'll get over it.
JACKY. I've done something else wrong, too. I've stolen something.
MARTHA. Miss Jacky!
JACKY. Yes, I have—my school report. It came by the second post. I recognized the envelope. Miss Eames always sends it to Uncle Philip and he reads it and forwards it to Nairobi. I didn't feel very *confident* about it, so I opened it.
MARTHA. That was very wrong of you, Miss Jacky. What did it say?
JACKY. It said "Conduct—fair. Lacks concentration and perseverance. Could do much better if she applied herself to the task at hand. Apt to be forgetful and careless." Forgetful and careless!

That's a nice thing to have said about me at a time like this, isn't it?

MARTHA (*crossing above the sofa to the table, where she tidies up*) Well, you'd better stick down the envelope again and put it back with the other letters.

JACKY. I can't. I tore it up and burnt it! Fancy sending out school reports a week before Christmas—even the Nazis didn't do things like that!

MARTHA (*behind the table*) All the same, it wasn't honest!

JACKY. I know, but I've decided *not* to be honest in future. In fact, I think I've decided to live an immoral life. I wish I'd started yesterday and not told them about the football pool.

(RUTH *enters up* L)

RUTH. Oh, here you are, Martha. I think we'll have tea in the dining-room. Would you like an egg, Jacky? Oh, dear, I forgot, there isn't one.

MARTHA. Yes, ma'am.

(MARTHA *goes out up* L. RUTH *crosses towards the fire*)

RUTH (*with forced brightness*) And what have *you* been doing all the afternoon?

JACKY. Just sitting, Aunt Ruth—just sitting!

RUTH. Oh. Oh, I see. (*She takes some knitting from the mantelpiece and sits at the top end of the sofa*)

JACKY (*after a pause*) Aunt Ruth! I'm sorry.

RUTH. Yes, dear. I know you are, but don't keep saying so. It's so irritating when people keep on saying the same thing over and over again.

JACKY. I'm sorry.

RUTH. Well, really.

JACKY. I'm so—— Oh, lord, I nearly said it again!

RUTH. Your uncle not back yet?

JACKY. No.

RUTH. I thought he'd be in before this.

JACKY. I expect he went all the way to Paddington with Grandma and saw her safely in the train. I hope so.

RUTH. Yes, so do I; I mean—— (*She laughs with* JACKY)

JACKY (*after a pause*) That's the one bright spot, isn't it—Grandma going?

RUTH. Certainly not. We're all very upset—very upset, indeed.

JACKY. Martha was saying just now that everybody's to be honest.

RUTH. Well?

JACKY. Nothing. I was just thinking.

RUTH. You're getting much too big a girl, Jacky, for *thinking*.

(*There is the sound of a door-slam off*)

Ah, here's your uncle. (*She listens*) Yes, he seems to be alone.

(PHILIP *comes in from up* L, *taking off his overcoat*)

PHILIP. Hello, Ruth! Hello, Jacky!

(JACKY *jumps up and crosses to him*)

RUTH. Everything *all right*?

PHILIP. Perfectly. What have you been doing with yourself, Jacky?

JACKY. Nothing much, Uncle Philip. (*She takes his hat and coat*)

RUTH. I'm afraid she's been thinking.

PHILIP (*up* LC) I've been thinking, too, Jacky, in the train coming down from Charing Cross. We haven't had your school report yet. I must send off my monthly letter to Nairobi in a day or two. I'd better ring Miss Eames and ask her to send it along so that I can enclose it.

JACKY. Oh, lord!

(JACKY *hurries out of the room up* L. PHILIP *crosses slowly above the table towards the fire*)

RUTH (*after a pause*) Grandma's gone?

PHILIP (*at the fire*) Yes.

RUTH. You took her across to Paddington?

PHILIP. Yes.

RUTH. And saw her into the train?

PHILIP. Yes.

RUTH. I'm glad. It would be dreadful if—anything happened to her.

PHILIP. It won't. She had a corner seat, back to the engine, and when I left there was only one other woman in the carriage.

RUTH. It's rather a relief, I must say.

PHILIP. Not half. (*Suddenly*) I say, old girl.

RUTH. What?

PHILIP. I couldn't sleep last night——

RUTH. It was hardly likely you *would*.

PHILIP. No, I don't mean about the money. It was about you and me quarrelling. You were quite right about Bournemouth.

RUTH. Bournemouth?

PHILIP. Yes. I saw it all clearly. It wasn't much for you to ask —to be able to spend the rest of your life at a seaside resort with a tea chalet on the beach. You were quite right. I *was* brutal. And selfish, too!

RUTH. No, no, dear, it was *my* fault.

PHILIP. No. It was *mine*.

RUTH. It was wrong of me to expect a man of your age, a man with not many years to live, to give up all his friends and resign from the golf club.

PHILIP. I shall have to do that anyway.

RUTH. Oh, Philip, I'm so sorry!

PHILIP. It's all right, old thing. Of course, it's an awful disappointment—about the pool, but—well, we shall manage all right.

(MARTHA *enters up* L)

Yes, Martha, what is it?

MARTHA (*crossing to behind the top end of the sofa*) This note, sir. By hand. It's just come. (*She hands him a note*)

PHILIP. Thank you, Martha.

(MARTHA *exits up* L)

What on earth—I seem to know the writing. (*Inspecting it carefully*) Whoever can it be?

RUTH. Why not open it?

PHILIP. Eh? Oh yes. (*He opens the note and reads*) Well, I never did! Ruth. It's all right!

RUTH. What, dear?

PHILIP. It's all right. Everything's all right. Listen to this:

(RUTH *looks up enquiringly*)

It's from the golf club. (*He reads*) "Dear Stafford, I received your letter tendering your resignation this morning and duly placed it before the Committee. They were deeply grieved to hear of your decision and feel that, in the circumstances, it was quite impossible for them to accept same. It was decided unanimously that, as a token of appreciation of your good service to the club in past years, you should be invited to become an honorary member. Sincerely . . ." Can you beat that?

RUTH. Honorary member? Does that mean you don't pay any subscription?

PHILIP. Yes.

RUTH. There you are, you see. And you were going to waste seventy-five pounds!

PHILIP (*re-reading the letter*) I say, this is wonderful. D'you know, I don't care now if—— (*Suddenly*) Sorry, dear, it won't help you to get to Bournemouth, will it?

RUTH (*pretending ignorance*) Bournemouth? Never mind, dear. I don't suppose I should really have wanted to leave when it came to the point.

PHILIP (*after moving close to her*) D'you know, you're a damned good wife. Don't let's ever quarrel again.

RUTH. I hope not, dear. (*She kisses him*)

PHILIP (*moving slowly around the top end of the sofa to* RC) I don't suppose I meant what I said about not winning the money, but it's had its advantages. The chief one is that it's stopped Denis from making a fool of himself. Thank heavens, Jacky spoke up before he was ass enough to send that cheque.

RUTH. Of course, dear. You know best.

PHILIP. I only wish Denis thought so, too. He hasn't said any more about leaving, has he?

RUTH. No, dear.

PHILIP. He can be an obstinate young devil at times.

RUTH. Yes. He takes after you in so many ways. Everybody says so.

PHILIP. I'm not obstinate.

RUTH. No, dear, I meant ...

(*There is the sound of a door banging off*)

Here is Denis! If you take my advice, Philip, I shouldn't say anything about it. Just go on as if nothing has happened.

PHILIP. Bit difficult! However, I'll try.

(*The door up* L *opens and* DENIS *enters. He looks tired and despondent*)

RUTH. Hello, dear! (*She rises and crosses to him*)

(PHILIP *remains* LC)

DENIS. Hello, Mother! (*Rather coldly to Philip*) 'Evening, Dad.

PHILIP (*falsely gay*) Good evening, Denis.

RUTH. I must go and help Martha. We're having tea in the dining-room—when it's ready.

DENIS. I shan't be in to tea. I have to go out again.

RUTH. Oh dear, what a pity! However, I expect you know best. (*She goes towards the door and returns*) Try and cheer up, dear. Your father says it's a good thing you haven't won the money. You'd only have done something silly.

(RUTH *goes out up* L. DENIS *goes straight to the phone and lifts the receiver*)

DENIS. Long Acre four-three-one-nine, please.

(PHILIP *recognizes the number and looks startled*)

No. One—nine.

PHILIP. I say, Denis ...

DENIS (*coldly*) Yes? What is it?

PHILIP. I—nothing. (*He sits* R *of the table, takes out his pipe and commences to fill it*)

DENIS (*after a pause, speaking into the receiver*) Hello, is that you, Eric? ... Eh? Who's that speaking? ... Is Mr Tranter there? ... What? ... Who am I? ... A friend of his and I want to speak ... (*Getting annoyed*) And who are you, for that matter? ... My name? ... I want to speak to Mr Tranter ... Oh, he isn't. Why the devil couldn't you say so at first? ... No, I'll ring again. (*He puts down the receiver. It is obvious that he is in a bad temper. He takes a cigarette from his case*)

PHILIP (*who is lighting his pipe*) Light? (*He offers a match*)

DENIS (*coldly*) It's all right, thanks. (*He tries to light his cigarette with a lighter but it won't light*)
PHILIP (*watching him struggle*) Better try a match, old son. (*He rises and holds out a box*)
DENIS (*taking it reluctantly*) Thanks. (*He lights his cigarette and returns the matches*)
PHILIP. Thanks.

(DENIS *sits in the chair* L *of the table and pulls a newspaper from his pocket.* PHILIP *strolls away towards the fire, his back to* DENIS)

(As DENIS *opens the paper*) Any news?
DENIS (*offering Philip the paper*) Here you are!
PHILIP (*turning*) No, I meant—any news at the office?
DENIS. I don't know. I haven't been. I've been trying to raise that other three-fifty.
PHILIP (*upset*) But I thought—— Oh, I see.
DENIS. You thought it was all off, I suppose? Well, it isn't yet! I thought it was all off, too, when Jacky told us about the coupon, but, after I'd gone into it thoroughly in my mind, I didn't see why it should be. It only meant I was back to where I was on Saturday night. I've been around to a few pals in the city to see if I could raise the necessary.
PHILIP. Have you succeeded?
DENIS. I've raised a hundred of it. And I think I've got another hundred too. Charlie Denver's half promised to put in the balance of his gratuity, too. He's going to let me know for certain this evening. If he's on then I write another cheque to Eric, and it goes off tonight. I'll chance raising the balance before Thursday.
PHILIP (*moving a couple of paces in from the fire to down* RC) I don't think that's at all wise, involving your friends in a thing like that.
DENIS. That's my look-out. And theirs, too.
PHILIP. Very well, my boy, I can't stop you. (*He goes away again to the fire*) I say! (*He hesitates*) You didn't mean what you said about clearing out, did you—leaving Caterham? (*He is looking into the fire, his back to Denis*)
DENIS. Yes, I did. I've phoned Eric half a dozen times today about the room but he seems to be out. There's some chap there I don't know.
PHILIP. It seems a pity just because we disagreed on a point of business—that you should leave home.

(DENIS *does not answer*. PHILIP *turns*)

Your mother will be frightfully upset.
DENIS. It can't be helped. I'm sorry, Dad. It was a mistake for me to come back here after I was demobbed. It's not your fault but you can't help treating me as if I was a kid and I don't intend to wear it.

PHILIP (*half pleading*) Can't we leave the situation alone for a day or two and see what happens?

DENIS. If you like, but I don't think I shall change my mind. (*He moves up* L *to the door*) I'm going over to see Charlie Denver. He'll be in by now. If Eric rings, tell him I'll be back in half an hour or less.

(DENIS *opens the door as* JACKY *enters*)

Hello, Jacky.

(PHILIP *sits at the top end of the sofa*)

JACKY. Denis, I'm terribly sorry . . .

DENIS. For heaven's sake, forget it, kid. No good crying over spilt milk. (*He notices how miserable* JACKY *looks*) Come on, now cheer up! We're not sunk yet—not by a long chalk.

(DENIS *goes out*)

JACKY (*coming down to the fire*) Uncle Philip?

PHILIP. Yes, Jacky?

JACKY. You said you were going to ring Miss Eames about my report.

PHILIP. I'll do it later on this evening.

JACKY. There's no need. It's come!

PHILIP. What has?

JACKY. My report.

PHILIP. Good. Where is it then?

JACKY. It's rather difficult to explain. (*She hesitates*)

PHILIP. I see. Well, have a shot at it.

JACKY. It was like this. It came with a lot of other letters and I'm afraid I opened it—accidentally.

PHILIP. Oh, well, it doesn't matter. I should have shown it to you, anyway.

JACKY. Then—I was reading it and I dropped it and it fell into the fire and was burnt.

PHILIP. I see.

JACKY. Unfortunate, wasn't it?

PHILIP. Very. A lot of unfortunate things seem to be happening to you this weekend, Jacky, don't they?

JACKY. Yes. (*In a small voice*) Don't they?

PHILIP. Did you read it?

JACKY. Oh, yes.

PHILIP. That's all right, then. I can tell your father what it said.

JACKY (*moving across the top end of the sofa to* RC) I don't remember all the details.

PHILIP. The final summary will be enough. Conduct and all that. What did it say?

JACKY. It said "Conduct—excellent. A great improvement all round."

PHILIP (*smiling to himself*) Good! Your father will be pleased to hear that.

JACKY. Yes, won't he?

PHILIP. And a bit surprised, too! I mean—after last term. All right, Jacky, I'll tell him.

JACKY. Thank you. (*She goes up* L *to the door. Then she turns and comes back to behind the sofa*) Uncle Philip!

PHILIP. Yes, Jacky?

JACKY. Would you like to know what it *really* said?

PHILIP. You've just told me.

JACKY. No, I haven't. It said "Conduct very bad indeed. This girl is a liar, a cheat and a complete louse."

PHILIP. Dear me! As bad as that?

JACKY. Very nearly. (*She runs around the top end of the sofa and kneels at his feet*) Oh, Uncle Philip, I'm so sorry!

PHILIP (*taking her hands*) That's all right.

JACKY. I don't think I'm very good at villainy. I should have felt awful if you'd believed me.

PHILIP. You needn't have worried, Jacky. I didn't!

JACKY. D'you know, Uncle Philip, you're rather a deceptive character—you're not half so innocent as you seem.

PHILIP. Perhaps my natal innocence has been soiled by circumstances, Jacky.

JACKY. They won't be very pleased with that report in Nairobi. (*She hesitates*) I don't suppose you could ... (*She stops*)

PHILIP. Withhold the information from the outposts of the Empire?

(JACKY *nods*)

Suppose I say that Jacky's school report is much the same as usual? Do you think that will be sufficiently vague?

JACKY. You're an awfully decent type, Uncle Philip. I often wonder why you have such a forgiving nature.

PHILIP. Practice, I expect.

(CAROL *enters up* L. JACKY *rises and goes to the fire*)

CAROL (*coming to the back of the sofa*) Father, I've just thought of something. Sorry to refer to an unhappy subject, Jacky, but it's important.

PHILIP. What is it?

CAROL. Those telegrams we sent off to Imperials—claiming the prize. (*She hesitates*)

PHILIP. Well?

CAROL. They can't bring a case against us, can they? Attempting to obtain money under false pretences!

PHILIP. Of course not. It was a genuine mistake.

E

CAROL. Yes, but how do they know it was a mistake? I read something the other day about a man who tried to cheat a bookmaker and was sent to prison.

PHILIP. I don't think we've any cause for anxiety, Carol.

JACKY. If anyone has to go to prison it had better be me.

CAROL. But *I* sent the telegram.

PHILIP. So did I! *And* Denis.

CAROL. And Mother, too!

PHILIP. That's all right, then. We shall all be able to play bridge in the Black Maria.

CAROL. I don't think it's a joking matter . . .

PHILIP. Well, I do. Forget all about it.

(MARTHA *enters up* L *and comes to* C *above the table*)

Yes, Martha?

MARTHA. There's a gentleman to see you, sir. I think he's a policeman, sir!

CAROL (*gasping*) A policeman!

PHILIP (*rising, a little shaken*) What makes you think that, Martha?

MARTHA. I don't know, sir. But he's got a *real* policeman with him—in uniform—one of the locals, sir.

CAROL. Father, I . . .

PHILIP. It's all right, Carol—leave this to me. I expect I shall be able to explain. (*To Martha*) Show the gentleman in.

MARTHA. Yes, sir.

(MARTHA *exits up* L)

PHILIP. Now then, Carol. You and Jacky push off. (*He passes Jacky over to* RC)

CAROL. But . . .

PHILIP (*shooing them off*) Do as I tell you.

(*They move up* L *towards the door*)

And for heaven's sake, Carol, don't breathe a word of this to your mother. If she comes rushing in to try and save the situation we'll all get ten years.

CAROL. Very well, Father.

(CAROL *goes out with* JACKY.

PHILIP *crosses to the fireplace and adopts what he considers to be a nonchalant pose. He tries to hum a tune.* MARTHA *opens the door and shows in* GEORGE KIRBY. KIRBY, *who is a detective, is a fresh-complexioned, heavily-built man of about forty. He wears neat clothes, a dark overcoat and carries his hat. His manner is civil but direct*)

KIRBY. Good evening, sir.

PHILIP (*at the fire*) Good evening.

KIRBY (*just inside the door*) Sorry to trouble you.

PHILIP. Not at all. Come in.
KIRBY. Thank you, sir.

(KIRBY *comes down* C *as* MARTHA *exits and closes the door*)

PHILIP (*meeting Kirby downstage in front of the table*) Won't you sit down, Mr——?
KIRBY. Kirby's my name, sir. Thank you. *You* are Mr Stafford?
PHILIP. I am.
KIRBY. Then perhaps I'd better show you this, sir. Just to establish my identity. (*He shows Philip a police officer's identity card*)
PHILIP (*reading it*) Criminal Invest—— I see. (*He returns the card*) Well, sit down all the same, Mr Kirby.
KIRBY. Thank you. (*He sits* L *of the table*)
PHILIP. What about your—er—friend——

(KIRBY *gives him an enquiring look*)

—the chap outside?
KIRBY. Eh? Oh, he can stay where he is—for the present. Now, Mr Stafford, I'm making enquiries regarding a certain matter and I'm afraid it will be my duty to have to ask you a few questions.
PHILIP (*sitting* R *of the table*) Certainly, Inspector, but I must say, at the outset, that I consider the whole thing is laughable.
KIRBY. In what way, sir?
PHILIP. Scotland Yard being dragged into a trivial affair like this.
KIRBY. I'm afraid that Headquarters don't regard it as being at all trivial. On the contrary, it's a matter of extreme gravity.
PHILIP. I should have thought it was bad enough that we don't get the money.
KIRBY. So you were *expecting* to make a good deal out of it?
PHILIP. A few thousand, at least.
KIRBY. I see. (*He makes a note in his book*)
PHILIP. Isn't it bad enough that the whole thing has fallen down on us?
KIRBY. I'm afraid not. (*He goes on writing*)
PHILIP. I can assure you, Inspector, that any telegram—all the telegrams, in fact—were sent off in perfectly good faith. Before we realized that there had been a slip-up.
KIRBY. You mean, before you knew that the *police* were interested in the matter?
PHILIP. Naturally.
KIRBY. I see. (*He makes a further note*)
PHILIP (*rising and moving to above the table*) I suppose I might have sent another wire directly I found out Jacky's mistake, but we were so upset . . .
KIRBY. Jacky! Who's Jacky?
PHILIP. My niece.

KIRBY. I really can't see what *she* has to do with it.

PHILIP (*coming round to* L *of Kirby*) But it was Jacky's mistake that's caused the whole bother. She forgot to post the damned thing!

KIRBY. What damned thing?

PHILIP. The coupon, of course.

KIRBY. Coupon?

PHILIP. The football coupon! (*He sits in the desk chair facing Kirby*) Now, look here, Inspector, it was a genuine mistake. I heard the results on the wireless and we checked them up with a London newspaper. The telegrams were sent off and it wasn't until some hours later that Jacky confessed that she hadn't posted the coupon. *Now*, do you see?

KIRBY (*getting up*) No. (*He moves below the table and turns*) You *are* Mr Stafford, aren't you?

PHILIP. Of course I am. So you needn't try to get me muddled about my own name. It's Stafford—Philip Stafford.

KIRBY. Philip Stafford? Not *Denis*?

PHILIP. Of course not. Denis is my son.

KIRBY. Oh, I see! I beg your pardon, Mr Stafford, I'm talking to the wrong man. It's your *son* I want to see. Where is he?

PHILIP. He's just slipped out for a few minutes. He should be back any time now.

KIRBY. In that case I'd better wait. (*He sits again* L *of the table*)

PHILIP. Then all this has nothing to do with the football pool?

KIRBY. Of course not. I've no time to waste on things like that.

PHILIP. Then why do you want to speak to Denis? (*Suddenly*) He hasn't been getting himself into some sort of mess, has he?

KIRBY. That's what I have to find out, Mr Stafford.

PHILIP (*very disturbed*) But Denis is such a sound sort of lad, Inspector. Nobody could wish for a better son. He's just out of the Air Force and—— (*Suddenly rising*) I know where he is. I'd better go and warn him—er—fetch him . . .

KIRBY. *Warn* him?

PHILIP. I mean, explain to him that you're here.

KIRBY. I'd rather do the explaining myself.

PHILIP. But—— (*He breaks off*) Is it *serious*?

KIRBY. It may be. It all depends.

PHILIP. This is awful! Now, look here, Inspector——

(PHILIP *breaks off as there is the sound of a kick and slam off stage*)

KIRBY. Is that him?

PHILIP. Sounds like it. I'll go and—— (*He moves towards the door*)

KIRBY. Stay where you are, please, sir.

(*The door slams.* PHILIP *sits again, down* L *as* DENIS *comes in up* L)

DENIS (*moving towards the fire behind the table*) I say, Dad——

(*He breaks off as he sees Kirby*) Sorry, I didn't know anyone was here.

KIRBY. It's all right.

PHILIP (*rising*) This gentleman—Mr Kirby—he wants to speak to you, Denis. He's a police inspector.

DENIS (*obviously shaken*) A police inspector?

KIRBY. Yes, sir. (*He shows his identity card*)

PHILIP. I think he wants to ask you some questions about——

KIRBY (*interrupting briskly*) That's all right, sir. I'll do the talking if you don't mind. (*To Denis*) Won't you sit down?

DENIS. I—yes, of course. (*He sits R of the table*)

KIRBY. I don't think I need detain you any longer, Mr Stafford.

PHILIP. I'm staying here.

KIRBY. But . . .

PHILIP. This is my house, Inspector, and I intend to do what I please in it. (*He sits down deliberately in the desk chair*)

KIRBY. Very well, sir. Just as you like. Only I must warn you that there must be no obstruction of any sort. (*To Denis*) Your name is Stafford—*Denis* Stafford?

DENIS. Yes.

KIRBY (*rising and crossing to the fire*) Then, perhaps you'll be able to assist me in some enquiries I'm making. (*He opens his notebook*)

DENIS. I'll try.

KIRBY. Thank you. First of all, have you any knowledge of an Ordnance Dump situated near Little Norby in Berkshire?

DENIS. Good Lord! So it's about *that*, is it?

KIRBY. So you *do* know something about it?

DENIS (*nervously*) I—I've *heard* of it, certainly.

KIRBY. What have you heard?

DENIS. That there was a lot of Government property there. It's been there for years. Nothing unusual about *that*, eh?

KIRBY (*ignoring this*) Did you know that most of the material consists of motor tyres and spare parts?

DENIS. Yes. I was told so.

KIRBY. Do you know a man named Radshaw?

DENIS. No, I've never met him.

KIRBY. But you know of him?

DENIS. I believe he's a cousin of a friend of mine, Eric Tranter.

KIRBY. Then you admit you know Eric Tranter? When did you see him last?

DENIS. Two or three days ago. Friday, I believe it was.

KIRBY. But you've spoken to him on the telephone since?

DENIS. I may have done.

KIRBY. You've telephoned him two or three times today, haven't you?

DENIS. Yes. But I haven't *spoken* to him today. He wasn't in.

KIRBY. No. Each time you've rung up you've spoken to a

colleague of mine. It may interest you to know that Eric Tranter was arrested late last night.

Denis (*thoroughly alarmed*) What!

Kirby. And his cousin, Captain Radshaw, at the same time.

Denis. On what charges?

Kirby. In the case of Radshaw—theft!

Philip. Theft?

Kirby. Yes, Mr Stafford. Theft of Government property on a very large scale. In the case of Tranter, the charge is receiving and conspiracy.

Denis. Good lord! (*He recovers*) Well, of course, if I can *help* you in any way, I will.

Kirby. I suggest that you were a partner of Tranter's.

Denis. Nonsense.

Kirby (*moving below the sofa and standing leaning against its back*) Now, Mr Stafford, if I were you I shouldn't try to bluff this out. We know far too much for that.

Denis. What do you mean?

Kirby. I mean that we've known all about Captain Radshaw and the Little Norby place for the past three weeks or so. It was obvious, too, that there were other people implicated besides Radshaw. D'you see?

Denis. I still say it's nothing to do with me. If Tranter said I was mixed up in it, he was lying.

Kirby. He didn't.

Denis. There you are, you see!

Kirby. Unfortunately, though, when the police are dealing with matters like this they sometimes resort to—well, methods you might consider ungentlemanly.

Denis. Such as?

Kirby. Such as tapping telephone wires.

Denis. Good God! (*He half rises and sits again*)

Kirby. That puts rather a different complexion on it, doesn't it? Yesterday morning you had a conversation with Tranter . . .

Denis. It was about a spare room in his house and . . .

Kirby. No. It was about something entirely different. (*He consults his notebook*) You told Tranter that you were "in" on his project. You promised to let Tranter have a hundred and fifty pounds. He was to have it first thing this morning. You were sending off the cheque together with a draft agreement last night —for certain.

Denis. I didn't send it!

Kirby. You were very emphatic about it on the telephone.

Denis. I—changed my mind.

Kirby. You mean you knew all the time that the business was crooked?

Denis. I mean nothing of the sort. Tranter told me his cousin had bought the stuff. I had no idea it was stolen.

KIRBY (*moving around back of the table to* L *of Denis*) Do you expect me to believe that you thought a deal of this nature could be based on honest bona-fide trading?

DENIS. Yes.

KIRBY. Did you take any steps to find out if the business was being run on honest lines?

DENIS. No.

KIRBY (*returning to his former position, his back to the sofa*) You were prepared to invest five hundred pounds in this scheme and send off an immediate cheque for one hundred and fifty pounds without making the slightest effort to verify the details or satisfy yourself that the transaction was an honest one?

DENIS. Well—yes—I—I suppose so.

PHILIP (*rising*) Really, Inspector, you must remember that Denis is young and——

KIRBY. Mr Stafford, I've already warned you to keep silent. I hold a warrant for your son's arrest and if you obstruct me then I shall have no alternative other than to use it and continue the investigation somewhere else.

PHILIP. Arrest? You're not serious.

KIRBY. I am. (*To Denis*) Why didn't you investigate the matter?

DENIS. I've already told you.

KIRBY. Did you refrain from thoroughly investigating this thing because you *had* suspicions and thought it was wiser not to find out the truth?

DENIS. I—I—— (*He hesitates*)

KIRBY. Well? Surely you can answer that?

PHILIP. *I* can!

KIRBY. Mr Stafford!

PHILIP (*crossing in front of the table to Kirby*) But you want the truth and I can tell you the truth. I can explain the whole thing. Will you allow me to speak?

KIRBY (*after a pause*) All right. (*He moves back to the fire*)

PHILIP. I was here yesterday when Denis was talking to Tranter on the telephone. Before he rang Tranter, Denis told me the whole story. He asked my advice. I think he had some idea that there might be something wrong somewhere, and I told him that, in my opinion, everything was fair and above board. I reassured him and said I would take the responsibility. I even offered to put up the balance of the money, so if you're going to arrest him, you'd better arrest me, too! After Denis had rung Tranter on our joint behalf he changed his mind and decided to have nothing to do with it. *Now* are you satisfied?

KIRBY. I might be if you had any proof of that.

PHILIP (*down* RC) But you have your proof. You've occupied Tranter's rooms and if Denis sent that cheque it would be in your possession.

KIRBY. It didn't turn up this morning, but your son may have missed the post.

PHILIP. In that case, it would turn up by the next. Ring up and find out.

KIRBY. Very well. (*He goes above the table to the telephone and lifts the receiver*) Give me Long Acre four-three-one-nine.

(*There is a pause, during which* PHILIP *exchanges looks with* DENIS *and retreats to the fire*)

Is that you, Metcalfe? Kirby here. I'm speaking from Caterham. Tell me—is the afternoon post in yet . . . It is? Good! Has that cheque written by Denis Stafford turned up yet? . . . Oh, I see! All right, good-bye. (*He replaces the receiver*)

PHILIP. Well?

KIRBY. It hasn't arrived.

PHILIP (*moving to above the table*) Then that ends the whole matter?

KIRBY (*down* L) Well, I don't know . . .

PHILIP. You can't arrest anyone for *intention*. The whole thing depends on that cheque having been sent—on your having it in your possession.

KIRBY. I suppose it does—in a way.

PHILIP. There's no "in a way" about it. Without that cheque you've no proof of anything and the cheque was never written.

KIRBY (*coming up to Philip*) All right, Mr Stafford. In the circumstances, I'm prepared to let the matter drop. Of course, if that cheque turns up later it will be a very different cup of tea.

DENIS. There's no chance of that. (*He rises and crosses* RC)

KIRBY. For your sake, I hope it won't. (*He puts away his notebook*)

PHILIP (*above the table*) Will you have a drink before you go, Inspector?

KIRBY. Thank you, sir, but I must be getting along.

(KIRBY *moves towards the door. As he reaches it,* RUTH *rushes in*)

RUTH. Oh, good evening! (*She rushes past Kirby to* C) Carol has just told me. There's an awful policeman here. (*She turns back to Kirby*) I'm so sorry but have *you* seen an awful policeman?

KIRBY. I'm afraid I *am* the awful policeman!

RUTH. Oh, dear me! What have I said? You really must excuse me. I mean, you look so respectable—I had no idea—I didn't mean that you were awful personally, only that . . .

PHILIP. For heaven's sake, Ruth!

RUTH. What's the matter? I haven't said anything to make things blacker, have I?

DENIS. Mother!

RUTH. I think the only thing to do is to make a clean breast of it.

KIRBY (*with sudden renewed interest*) Clean breast of *what*, Madam?

RUTH. Why, the whole thing, of course. It was obvious they'd all get found out in the end.

KIRBY. I see. In view of what you've said—— (*He remembers and turns to Philip*) I suppose, sir, this has nothing to do with a football pool?

PHILIP. But, of course!

KIRBY. In that case, I'll be moving along. Good evening, sir. (*He turns up* L *towards the door*)

RUTH. Then you're not going to arrest anyone?

KIRBY. No, madam.

RUTH. I'm so glad. I was going to suggest that my husband should bribe you, but I see now it's not necessary.

KIRBY. I'll be—— (*To Philip*) If you'll forgive me saying so, sir, I don't think the police can do much in this house. What we really require is a commissioner for lunacy. Good evening!

(KIRBY *goes out up* L, *followed by* RUTH)

RUTH (*as they go*) You must have something before you go, Inspector—have an egg!

DENIS (*mopping his brow*) Crumbs! (*He rushes upstage to Philip*) I say, Dad, you thumping old liar!

PHILIP. Eh?

DENIS. All that about you having advised me to go in with Eric against my better judgement. Gosh, but you saved me from a crash all right. I was getting so tied up that I might have said anything. And then stepping in about the cheque not having been sent!

PHILIP. I thought you hadn't sent it. Of course, it all happened yesterday and I didn't quite remember.

DENIS. Dad, a lot of things happened yesterday that I'd rather not remember.

PHILIP. Same here, old son. Thank God you didn't send that cheque.

DENIS. Not half. And the awful thing is that I was going to send it off tonight.

PHILIP. Near thing, eh?

DENIS. To adopt Jacky's picture parlance—sez you!

(CAROL *rushes into the room from up* L)

CAROL. Father! For heaven's sake do something!

PHILIP. What's up now?

CAROL. It's mother. I believe she's been arrested!

PHILIP. What?

CAROL. She's out by the gate with that policeman. She seems terribly excited about something.

PHILIP. Oh, for heaven's sake . . .

(PHILIP *hurries out*)

CAROL (*to Denis*) What's happened?
DENIS. Everything's all right. No need to worry.
CAROL. Are you sure?
DENIS. Yes. It's only mother indulging in her natural flair for inappropriate conversation. (*He crosses up* R, *pulls one of the curtains open and opens the window*)

(MARTIN LATHAM *stands outside*)

What the deuce?
MARTIN. It's all right, Denis—it's only *me*!
DENIS. What the devil are you doing out there?
MARTIN. Waiting.
DENIS. What for?
MARTIN. To come in.
DENIS. Well, *come* in, then!
MARTIN. Thank you!

(MARTIN *enters.* CAROL *tosses her head and moves towards the door*)

Please don't go. I want to speak to you.

(CAROL *stops.* MARTIN *turns to Denis*)

Would it be asking too much to—leave us alone?
DENIS (*tactfully*) No. I want some air, anyway.

(DENIS *goes out through the window, turning up the collar of his jacket.* MARTIN *and* CAROL *stand staring at each other*—CAROL LC *and* MARTIN *by the window. There is a long pause*)

CAROL (*wildly*) Well, Martin, what is it?
MARTIN. I've been thinking.
CAROL. Have you?
MARTIN (*coming down* R *of the table*) Yes. I've been thinking all day—and all night, too.
CAROL (*coldly*) How exhausting for you!
MARTIN. Yes. Very. I feel quite worn out. (*He pauses*) Carol, did you mean what you said last night?
CAROL (*moving down to below* L *of the table*) What did I say last night?
MARTIN. You said you hated me. Did you mean it?
CAROL. I did.
MARTIN. And do you *still* hate me?
CAROL. Of course I do.
MARTIN. Oh, I see. (*Very deliberately he moves to her, seizes her in his arms and kisses her violently*)
CAROL (*struggling*) Martin! Let go! Martin! What are you doing?

MARTIN. Kissing you. (*He kisses her again*)

CAROL. Let me go, I tell you! (*Struggling*) Martin! Do you hear me? Let go! People can see us! I'll scream. (*She succeeds in freeing herself*) Have you gone mad?

MARTIN. No. On the contrary. I wanted to do that—to kiss you—for months, for years even—and I didn't dare risk it.

CAROL. Why not?

MARTIN. I thought you might be offended if I did. But, since you *hate* me, it doesn't matter, does it?

CAROL. I didn't say I hated you as much as all that!

MARTIN. What do you mean?

CAROL. Are you telling me you wouldn't have kissed me unless I'd said I hated you!

MARTIN. Exactly. Not unless we were engaged to be married. It wouldn't have been honourable.

CAROL (*taking a step towards him*) Martin?

MARTIN. Yes, Carol?

CAROL. Suppose I'd said I didn't hate you?

MARTIN. Then, as your fortune no longer stands between us, I should have asked you to marry me.

CAROL. Martin, I *don't* hate you!

MARTIN. But you said you did.

CAROL. I was telling a lie.

MARTIN. Oh dear, Carol. That was wrong of you.

CAROL. So now we're engaged?

MARTIN (*breaking away to* R) I suppose so.

CAROL. You don't sound very thrilled about it. (*She moves towards him*) *Do* you want to marry me or *don't* you?

MARTIN. Of course I do.

CAROL. Then kiss me, you fool!

MARTIN. Certainly. (*After a timid start he kisses her violently*)

CAROL (*gasping for breath*) Martin, darling! I had no idea you had it in you!

MARTIN. I'm sorry. When I'm roused I've a terribly passionate nature.

(CAROL *throws her arms around his neck and he kisses her again. The door opens and* RUTH *enters*)

RUTH (*coming down* R *of the table*) Carol! Martin! Well, really!

(MARTIN *jumps back*)

MARTIN. I beg your pardon, Mrs Stafford. I really didn't mean . . . (*He falls over the sofa back*)

CAROL. Of course you did! (*Coming behind the table*) It's all right, Mother, Martin and I are engaged.

RUTH. What! (*Delighted*) Oh, I'm so thankful. (*She goes to Martin and kisses him*) Martin! Dear boy! (*Going to kiss Carol*) Oh,

Carol, *what* a relief. How clever of you to bring him up to scratch *at last*!

CAROL. Mother!

RUTH. I must tell your father! (*She hurries up* L *to the door*) And Denis, too! And Jacky! (*She calls*) Philip!

PHILIP (*off*) What's up now?

(PHILIP *enters up* L)

RUTH (*up* R) It's Carol and Martin. They're engaged! Do hurry and congratulate him before he changes his mind.

PHILIP. I say, this is good news! (*He crosses to the sofa and shakes hands with Martin*) I'm delighted!

MARTIN. I suppose I should really ask you for your consent?

PHILIP. We can skip that. (*He crosses up* L *and kisses Carol*)

JACKY (*who has followed Philip into the room*) Well done, pal!

(JACKY *kisses* MARTIN, *who sits on the sofa, downstage end*)

MARTIN. Here! Here! I say——!

(JACKY *drops down below the fire*)

RUTH. Where's Denis? Denis must be told at once!

DENIS (*appearing in the window*) Told what?

RUTH. Wonderful news, dear. Carol and Martin are engaged!

DENIS. Wizard! (*He shakes hands with Martin*) 'Grats! (*Crossing to Carol*) So he's accepted you at last, eh?

(*The positions now are:* JACKY—*below the fire*, MARTIN—*on the lower end of the sofa*, PHILIP—RC, DENIS *and* CAROL—LC, RUTH —*down* L *of the table*)

CAROL. What!

PHILIP (*taking charge of the situation*) Well, this is a wonderful evening and no mistake about it, and the odd thing is that I suppose the person we have to thank for it is Jacky. When I think how miserable we all were yesterday morning, and how happy we all are tonight, I think everybody will agree that we owe Jacky a hearty vote of thanks.

DENIS. Hear! Hear!

CAROL. Good old Jacky!

MARTIN. Oh, dear, I've just remembered something. (*He rises*)

(*They all turn to him*)

I forgot all about this telegram. (*He takes a telegram from his pocket*) The boy must have left it at the wrong house. It's addressed to Stafford. (*He takes it to Philip*)

PHILIP. Let's have it! (*He takes it from Martin. He reads the telegram and his expression changes. There is a pause. He scratches his head*)

DENIS. What is it, Dad?

PHILIP. I can't make this out at all. I'm damned if I can.
CAROL. What does it say?
PHILIP (*reading slowly*) "Claim admitted. Dividend probably about twelve thousand. Congratulations. Imperials."
DENIS. Let me see. (*He takes the telegram and reads it*) Right enough.
PHILIP. But how can they possibly admit the claim when they haven't received the coupon?
DENIS. Beats me.
RUTH. Perhaps Jacky posted it after all.
PHILIP (*crossing to Jacky*) Have you still got it, Jacky?
JACKY (*producing the envelope*) Yes. Here it is.
PHILIP (*taking the envelope, moving* RC, *and showing it to the others*) Here it is! Here is the unposted coupon. You can't get away from that!
MARTIN. Excuse me, may I make a suggestion?
DENIS. You may!
MARTIN. Open it!

(PHILIP *opens the envelope and takes out a football pool form*)

PHILIP. No. Here it is! (*He shows it*) Here's the coupon all right.
MARTIN. May I see it?
PHILIP. Of course. (*He hands the coupon to Martin*)
MARTIN. Thank you. (*He examines the coupon*) I'm afraid you're not very observant, Mr Stafford—if you'll pardon me for saying so.
PHILIP. What do you mean?
MARTIN. This coupon is not for last Saturday's matches but for the Saturday before.
DENIS. What! (*He hurries over and snatches the coupon*) Give it to me!
MARTIN. It says quite distinctly "Matches to be played on December the fourteenth"—last Saturday was the twenty-first.
DENIS. Gosh! You're right! December the fourteenth.
PHILIP. But—I—I don't understand.
MARTIN. It was not last week's coupon Jacky omitted to post —it was the week's before.
PHILIP. Well, I'll be damned!
RUTH. Then we've won after all?
PHILIP. It looks like it.
DENIS. "Dividend probably about twelve thousand." That means four thousand apiece.
PHILIP. And thanks to Jacky, we have learned our lesson and will know what to do with it.
CAROL. Yes. Isn't it *splendid*, Martin?

(MARTIN *starts to move towards the door*)

(*Intercepting him*) Martin! Where are you going?

MARTIN. Abroad!
CAROL (*swinging him back on to the sofa*) Oh, no, you're not!
PHILIP. Well, this is a happy ending all right. Carol and Martin engaged, no more money worries for a bit. Denis safely out of a spot of trouble, and ...
JACKY. We've got rid of Grandma!

(GRANDMA *appears in the doorway up* L. *She wears bonnet and coat and carries a suitcase*)

GRANDMA. Oh, no, you haven't!

They all turn in amazement as—

the CURTAIN *falls*

PROPERTY PLOT

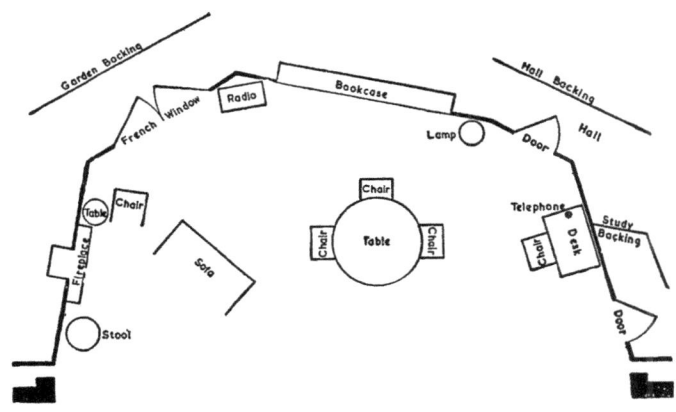

ACT I

On table c—Tea cloth
         6 plates
         6 knives
         Dish of buns (6)
         Plate of bread and butter
         Cups, saucers, etc.

On mantelpiece—Clock
              Spills
              Ashtrays
              Photographs
              Philip's pipe
              Matches

On stool (down R)—Evening newspapers
                     Ruth's knitting

On desk (down L)—Letters
                Pens
                Pencils
                Blotter
                Calendar
                Telephone
                Paper
                "Crib" for pool numbers (MARTIN)
                Engagement book
                Phone book

Below fireplace—Putter—used by PHILIP

Off stage—Teapot
          Hot-water jug
          Tray for clearing

Golf clubs (MARTHA)
Logs and Christmas cards (RUTH)
Unposted coupon (JACKY)
Coupon copy (PHILIP)
Cigarettes (CAROL)
Logs (RUTH)

ACT II

Alterations—Open curtains
　　　　　All Christmas cards on desk
　　　　　Alter clock to 10.30

On mantelpiece—Pipe
　　　　　　　　Matches

On sofa—Sunday papers

Off stage—Logs (MARTHA)
　　　　　Envelope (JACKY)
　　　　　Pipe and matches (PHILIP)
　　　　　Envelope (DENIS)
　　　　　Bowl of flowers and magazine (RUTH)
　　　　　Newspaper (CAROL)
　　　　　Christmas cards (RUTH)

ACT III

Alterations—Draw curtains
　　　　　Turn desk chair outwards
　　　　　Ashtray on table
　　　　　A few logs in grate
　　　　　Alter clock to 5.30

On armchair—Newspaper

On mantelpiece—Sewing

On table—Flowers

Off stage—Matches, pipe and tobacco (PHILIP)
　　　　　Telegram (MARTIN)
　　　　　Unstamped letter (MARTHA)
　　　　　Cigarettes, lighter and evening paper (DENIS)
　　　　　Police card and notebook (KIRBY)
　　　　　Letter (JACKY)
　　　　　Suitcase (GRANDMA)

EFFECTS REQUIRED THROUGHOUT PLAY

Telephone bell
Clock strike
Door slams

LIGHTING PLOT

ACTS I and III

Perches—2 1,000-watt spots—54 Pale Rose
Floats—51 Gold, 52 Pale Gold, 54 Pale Rose, 1 circuit each
Battens—1 circuit—54 Pale Rose
Firespot
Standard lamp
Fittings
Lengths
(Other spots, if available—51 Gold)

ACT II

Perches—2 1,000-watt spots—54 Pale Rose
Floats—As Act I
Battens—51 Gold, 52 Pale Gold, 54 Pale Rose—1 circuit each
Pagent spot through window
Firespot
Lengths
Standard lamp and fittings off
(Other spots, if available—51 Gold)

www.ingramcontent.com/pod-product-compliance
Ingram Content Group UK Ltd.
Pitfield, Milton Keynes, MK11 3LW, UK
UKHW021840210426
5322IPUK00022B/391